Easy-for-Me™ Reading
TEACHING MANUAL

from zero to reading in 77 self-paced lessons

by Sarah K Major, M.Ed.

Easy-for-Me™ Teaching Manual.

Grades Pre-K-1

ISBN: 978-1-936981-57-1

© 2007 Sarah Major
Printed in the United States of America

Published by: Child1st Publications LLC
800-881-0912

www.child1st.com
info@child1st.com

Moving Foreword

PURPOSE

Over the decades, the debate has raged over which method of teaching reading is most effective. New methods emerge, are rejected after a few years, are later recycled, all while a segment of our young population continues to emerge from 1st grade unable to read. These children are studied, sorted, and labeled in a variety of ways, and in many cases endure attempts at remediation. The number of high school students who cannot read seems to be growing despite the mandates and programs aimed at preventing such failure.

The purpose of this approach to teaching of reading is to provide a method consistent with how a child learns best so that every student has a chance of achieving success.

JUSTIFICATION

Many children seem unable to imbue abstract symbols with meaning, which is necessary for memory, recall, and the subsequent use of those symbols in meaningful ways. Many studies have been conducted on both the brain and learning, and on, more specifically, how the young child learns, but the results of these studies have not been applied to practice in such a way that methods of teaching reading have been significantly impacted in positive ways. Reading is still taught much the same way it has always been taught. The problem of illiteracy is widespread and significant, and without success in reading, children will become increasingly more at risk throughout their lives.

QUESTIONS

What is missing from our traditional approaches to teaching of reading? Research has shown that visual and kinesthetic modalities are powerful means of learning for young children. However, very few studies have been conducted to determine if the use of visual and kinesthetic connections between symbol and meaning, and the connection of the new elements of study to prior knowledge will significantly improve student ability to learn to read.

If breakdown in learning to read occurs in the area of meaning-making for abstract symbols (letters), is it possible that if visual and kinesthetic connections between symbol and meaning were used in teaching abstract symbols, and if each new concept were connected purposefully to prior knowledge, children would successfully learn to read?

I believe that if these connections are provided for all children (including at-risk children) they would experience success in learning to read. I further believe that if this type of method were used in regular kindergarten classrooms, most of the children who would have been at risk for reading would achieve success and thus avoid the discouragement of failure. It is not that this approach is primarily remedial; rather it operates in a way consistent with how a young child thinks and learns.

BACKGROUND & RESEARCH

According to Renate Nummela Caine and Geoffrey Caine in *Making Connections: Teaching and the Human Brain* (Addison Wesley 1994), one of the marvels of the human brain is its capacity for various types of memory. The work of Leslie Hart (*Human Brain and Human Learning*, Kent 1999) also explores the marvels of the body and brain connection. Various types of learning are stored in differing locations in the brain and body.

These "types" of learning include visual, kinesthetic, rhythmic/rhyming and so forth. Motions, which comprise the successful execution of a task, become so automatic that we are not even aware of thinking about how to perform these tasks. Examples include the art of riding a bicycle or playing a memorized song on the piano; skipping rope; dancing to music; or typing a paper. Each of these skills is comprised of myriad motions that combine fluidly into a smooth, rhythmic execution of task. Where are those memories stored? In the cerebellum. Once memories of body motions are stored in the cerebellum, they are powerful resources for memory recall.

Because visual stimuli are recalled with 90% accuracy, there is little more powerful than visual images for learning and recall, yet we often do not utilize this incredible tool in our teaching methods. Much is said about visual learners, and we think we have met these learners' needs when we provide certain lighting, colorful paper, pretty illustrations, and colored pens for them to write with.

It would be far more effective to provide images that are directly tied to the content/meaning we want the child to learn. These images become virtual snapshots which are stored in the visual spatial cortex. Instead of spending time trying to get a child to memorize a string of abstract symbols such as a series of letters in a word (which to the child might appear to be a mass confusion of forms) why not present the material in such a way that a snapshot is taken and stored instantly in memory? Easy in and easy to recall.

According to Leslie Hart and others, the brain is a pattern-seeking organ. A pattern may be an arrangement of form, such as a face that is familiar. The face of a child's mother, for example, is one of the most familiar patterns to a very young child. Other patterns, however, have become familiar to the child by the time she begins school. These patterns make up her prior knowledge - the context of all she is familiar with. According to Piaget, the young child is in the stage of development during which she deals primarily with the concrete world. She is not well equipped to deal with abstract or symbolic material (which is exactly what letters and numbers are). It is apparent, then, why using other avenues of learning is critical.

If we imbue the mysterious symbols that form our words with some sort of connection to tangible, visible, known elements from the child's own world, learning WILL occur. As a matter of fact, I have found that not only do children learn far more quickly, easily, and successfully, but they often don't even realize that they are learning. Learning through these modalities is like playing to young children.

In *Human Brain and Human Learning*, Leslie Hart states: "... assumptions have been made: that if a subject is fragmented into little bits, and the student is then presented with the bits in some order that seems logical to somebody, the student will be quite able to assemble the parts and merge with the whole - even though never having an inkling of the whole" (103). Somewhere, sometime, somebody determined that the proper sequence for teaching reading is to present a child with a series of ordered symbols (their ABCs), and ask him to memorize the symbols and later specific groupings of these symbols (words) so that he will be able to recall them rapidly and extract meaning from them. He is given no rationale for the necessity of learning these symbols, no context for the task, and no goal that would explain the point of the exercise.

Granted, some children have no problem digesting these 26 symbols, and can even sing-song a sample word and the sound that relates to each symbol.

For other children, the task is not only confusing and meaningless, but nearly impossible. For those children, 26 symbols, their matching sounds and sample words appear as a gigantic jumble of nonsense which adults earnestly desire them to "learn" and recall, and amazingly enough, make sense of and use. I picture an adult dropping a 1,000 piece jigsaw puzzle on the floor and asking a five year old to correctly assemble the picture those pieces represent.

In their book *Making Connections* the Caines speak of the "locale system" [O'Keefe and Nadel (1978)] which registers a continuous story of life experience [the prior knowledge or patterns of things familiar]. They claim, "the locale system must clearly be able to deal with rapid shifts in context and must also register an 'entire' context at a glance. One of its key features is its "indexing function" (47). They go on to state that if this indexing is to occur rapidly [indexing is the retrieving of facts and ideas from within that continuous story] there must be many strong connections, which contrast sharply with responses that are learned by rote (such as sequences of letters in spelling a word)..."(47).

The authors claim that these significant connections are made while learning from significant experience. "... new items become meaningful quickly by virtue of their being packaged in relevant, complex, and highly socially interactive experiences" (47).

The child must also have a rationale, be shown the "why" of learning symbols, and must see from the beginning how these symbols are used. There is a need for relevance, meaning, and excellent connections to the concrete world in order for many young children to make sense of this thing we call reading.

The Caines state: "That same memory system [the formation and use of thematic maps - O'Keefe and Nadel] is engaged when we use stories, metaphors, celebrations, imagery, and music, all of which are powerful tools for brain-based learning" (47). When a child is taught a first concept (for example: short sound for A) by using a story, a visual, and a meaningful body motion, a solid beginning is made.

An additional study that is marginally related to this one is "Promoting Conceptual Understanding Through Pictorial Representation," a study published by authors Kellah M. Edens and Ellen F. Potter in the Spring 2001 issue of *Reston*. The authors speak of Wittrock's (1989) generative theory which provides a "theoretical basis for promoting conceptual understanding (Mayer, Steinhoff, Bower, & Mars 1995)." They also make reference to Paivio's "dual-coding" theory (1990): "Specifically, Paivio (1990) argues that information is coded and represented both visually and verbally in memory. When information is coded in both visual and verbal systems with a correspondence between them, a generative process has occurred."

The authors are speaking of understanding and learning having a far broader base when there is more than one pathway to memory. We all know this. We have studied this in school and yet our knowledge has not reached far enough. We are still teaching reading the same old way.

FROM THEORY TO PRACTICE

In the Easy-for-Me™ Teaching Manual, the sound of A is introduced through visuals, story, and motion. Lesson 2 introduces the sound of T through a story that builds on the story of A and includes a visual and motion. Lesson 3 blasts the relevance issue into high gear by combining the two sounds into a word the child can read, write, and immediately use. The child is reading and writing his first word in Lesson 3! By Lesson 20, he will read his first book in the Easy-for-Me™ series!

The Easy-for-Me™ Reading Program is a careful blend of solid phonics instruction and sight word acquisition, combined with structural analysis of words. Add to that base an in-depth focus on phonemic awareness and manipulation, fluency and comprehension, and you have a recipe for success.

The Alphabet Teaching Cards provide young children with a visual reminder of the shape and sound for each letter by virtue of their design. Each letter is stylized to resemble a concrete, known object from the child's prior knowledge. For example, A is stylized to resemble an anthill. If a child were to close her eyes and conjure up an image of an anthill, the silhouette that would appear in her mind's eye would look like the silhouette of the symbol for capital A. The accompanying story explains how A came to be shaped like A rather than the little hill it started out being. No memorization is required. The story and the visual provide instant learning. Add the kinesthetic component by having the child "experience" the anthill by tenting her arms over her head mimicking the shape of capital A. The motion directly reflects the symbol being learned. Provide many more relevant connections by taking the child outside to see a real anthill, or constructing an antfarm together. You are building a rich context around the learning of the sound and shape of A, one that encompasses natural science.

SnapWords®: The sight word lists that we use are comprised of the Dolch list of words, Fry 300 words, and the Fountas and Pinnell 500 Frequently Recurring Words. All the words are stylized so the words themselves will resemble the meaning of the word. Not only is the visual image a means for learning and recall, but it shows the child that the word is a meaningful, understandable whole, not a string of symbols. Beyond that, the visual lends a rich meaning, a context, a real world connection to the word. Students passively learn that the reason we read is to distill meaning from the text and that reading goes far beyond word calling. Again, a rich context is provided for each word.

The Easy-for-Me™ Books are a critical tool in the learning to read process. Using this method, after learning only 8 sounds and two sight words (A and ON) children are able to decode/read two books! Adding 21 more sight words to the 8 sounds allows them to read a total of 7 books. They learn to USE their new knowledge before they have too many elements to manage. Decoding with only 8 sounds allows the child to focus on the skills of decoding and segmenting rather than on managing so many sounds and words. For those children who desperately need to know WHY they are learning something, being able to read a book will show them the reason. For those global learners, relevence means success.

The great good news is that the Easy-for-Me™ Teaching Manual is not only kid-friendly, but it is supremely teacher friendly because every little step is laid out for the teacher to follow. Just like we don't like to expect children to fill gaps left in the system, we don't like to leave gaps for teachers either. The experience is now complete. Join us, won't you, in moving into a new paradigm of learning made easy?

How to use this book:

PACE

The lessons in this manual are not meant to be taught in lock-step, one per day, nor the same amount of time spent on each lesson. Typically, at the beginning, lessons take longer, simply because the children are young and are confronting material that is highly symbolic and very new to them. The rule of thumb is to follow the demonstrated understanding of your child(ren). If they seem shaky, give them more time and more activities until they are ready to move on.

Do not be surprised if you start the manual at the beginning of the school year and it takes until Thanksgiving to reach Lesson 20. Sections 2 and 3 will go far more quickly as the skills needed for reading are mastered by the children. Learning and using those first 8 sounds will take by far the longest time.

APPROACH

Remember to approach the lessons with the attitude of making ideas and images available to the children, not one of teaching the material. Children learn little when they are asked to learn one detail after another. For example, if you decide "today we are going to learn the sight word WILL," learning the sight word WILL may or may not be a priority to the majority of your class. That is your agenda, not necessarily theirs. I would strongly recommend displaying a group (11-12) of stylized sight words attractively and accessibly placed so that children will be drawn to them on their own. They will gravitate towards the words that capture their fancy at any given moment. Follow their lead!

Of course, if today's lesson is to learn WILL, draw attention to the word from among the group of words displayed with it. Chances are, however, that if you have displayed a whole group of words for a few days, many of your children may already know the word. Especially if you have done some of the whole group activities for learning sight words. Bottom line: don't limit learning or direct too closely. Don't measure out the words one at a time. If we are willing to compromise, a lot will be gained. If today is the day for WILL, but Jeremy is really drawn to HERE and wants to talk about that word, likely he will learn both words if you are happy to accommodate his interests.

Our SnapWords® lists are broken into groups of 10-12 words for each list, which makes sharing a new group very easy for you.

Alphabet Tales

When reading the stories in *Alphabet Tales*, the air should be one of cuddling up to hear a favorite story. Read the designated story as expressively as possible, and let the children comment on what they notice as you are going through the story. When I read the story of A

to a kindergarten class, invariably we get about 3/4 of the way through the story and a handful of children will blurt excitedly, "It's an A, it's an A!" Rather than viewing this as disruptive, be excited with them as they are making meaning and connections in their learning.

The *Alphabet Tales* are great to use for practice in oral retelling. An effective homework assignment would be for each child to share the story with a parent at home.

INVENTED SPELLING IS TABOO

One of the most detrimental ideas to surface in the last several years was the notion that invented spelling is a natural stage for a child to pass through, which somehow magically will be abandoned once the child grows older and has more days in school. Or maybe reads more books.

When children first begin to record their thoughts and ideas on paper, their spelling is a mirror of the knowledge they have of words, sounds, and the structure of words to that point. Somehow, somewhere, the idea that invented spelling exists as a natural stage in a child's development turned into the idea that we should not tamper with the way a child spells when he is in this stage.

The more time I have spent working closely with children who fail at reading, the more I have seen the correlation between a lack of knowledge of the structure of words ("spelling") and a child's inability to read. I have worked with middle schoolers who were reading on a second grade level and failing miserably in all their courses because they could not read. Once I taught them the structure of words, sound spellings, they suddenly could read. They had discovered the patterns embedded in our language.

Children don't just magically absorb the structure of words. They have to be taught. Teaching children sound spellings and giving them practice in reading these sound spellings will directly result in their ability to decode unknown words. This process is begun in this series of lessons and will continue in *The Illustrated Book of Sounds & Their Spelling Patterns*.

JOURNALING

Starting in lesson 41, the practice of daily student journaling begins. Even very young children can begin to write a sentence or two and illustrate what they have written. It is critical for the teacher to review what the students have written and note the words the children do not know how to spell correctly. Beginning in Lesson 42, the teacher begins her center by reviewing journals. A mini-lesson that teaches the missing concept follows. If the concept is one that has surfaced throughout the classroom, it is best to teach the concept whole group during whiteboard time.

For example, if a child writes "My dog is osum," teacher will note that the child needs to know that AW says [sound of short] O. He also needs to have "sum" related to the sight words COME and SOME. It does not take long to show the group that when they write AWESOME, they will use the sound spelling AW and the sight word SOME. It is not going to stick in their brains if you leave it there, however. Generate other words that use the same sound spelling and have the children take a few minutes to write these words on their whiteboards. EX: LAW, JAW, FLAW, LAWN, DAWN, FAWN. What you will be doing is showing the children a pattern that repeats in our language--a pattern found in one word that applies to many others.

Then, when the children encounter a word with AW in their reading, they will recall the AW pattern they learned and will be able to read the unfamiliar word.

CONNECT READING AND WRITING

There is great value in guiding the children into the practice of writing as often as they read. If you start this practice early on, it will become as natural to them as breathing. For example, if you learn the sound for A, the follow-up activity is to let the children make A on whiteboards, then in an art project. Their doing the lesson from inside out will complete the necessary cycle of the lesson. In fact I would venture to say that learning will be minimal if the children have just listened to a lesson, or a story, but have not worked out the concept in a tangible way. If the children are learning to find words on a word wall, let them write the word they find on a whiteboard. Yes, it takes more time, but it is time spent in a way that will pay off in the long run.

FOCUS ON WHAT WORKS

Studiously avoid making each child's learning "look" the same. For example, not all children need the body motions equally. Frankly, some children will rely most on their visual senses to store away the concepts they are learning, but some children simply will not make it without using the body motions. When I teach this method, I encourage all the group to use the motions together during learning time, but then I pay close attention to which children seem to really need to use the motions as a means of recalling what they have learned. Some of my students literally could not decode for some months without using the motions for each letter as they decoded.

Remember, the motions are only tools to use if needed. Before I paint a room in my house, I go around removing tacks or nails from the walls that once held pictures. Before I bother to go fetch a hammer, I check to see if I can pull the nails out with my fingers. If I can, great! I save some steps. But if I need the hammer, I know where to find it.

The same thing goes for the motions. If a child is stuck and cannot say the sound for a letter symbol, or cannot name the sight word he's looking at, figure out if the motion prompt or the visual prompt will work best as a tool for remembering. The more visual children might need to hear you ask "What is shaped like this letter?" when looking at an M in order to remember that the M is like mountains. A kinesthetic learner will be able to recall the sound for M if you make the motion for the letter without saying anything at all.

LEARN LETTER SOUNDS

When teaching young children their ABC's, we don't teach letter names at all. We teach letter sounds because those are the bits children need to use in making words. For instance, we teach A as short-sound A as in cat...not AY as in day. We don't teach the name of T ("tea"); we teach the breathy, staccatto sound of t-t-t that comes at the beginning of "top." Words are made up of sounds, not letter names.

Some children become hopelessly lost in the process when they are asked to learn the letter names first, then learn the name of an object that represents each letter, THEN learn the sounds. They don't know how to manage all that information that, to them, seems unrelated and without purpose. If we simplify the process for them and let them understand that words are made of sounds (by segmenting short words for them) and those sounds are represented by symbols called letters, they will have far less to manage. They can understand that A is the picture of the sound of -a-. I've not met a child yet who did not pick up the letter names along the way, but I have met a lot of children who could read letter names but could not successfully decode a word.

SIX TYPES OF LESSONS

In order to provide a quick visual guide to the content of each lesson in this manual, we use the following symbols to identify the 6 types of lessons:

Sound. This symbol is used for a lesson header in which a sound is introduced. See Lesson 1 for an example.

Blend. This symbol is used for a lesson header in which students will blend sounds together. See Lesson 3 for an example.

Sight. This is used for a lesson header or a lesson section in which a sight word is being introduced. See Lesson 3.

Review. This is used for a lesson header when students will be reviewing material learned to date. See Lesson 18.

Read. This is used for a lesson header in which the children will be reading a new book. See Lesson 20.

Write. Although the children write in every lesson, this symbol is used for lesson headers in which there is a focus on writing. See Lesson 17.

SMALL GROUP INSTRUCTION

Small group instruction is the most effective way to meet the needs of the various learners in your room. If you are homeschooling, of course your instruction is automatically considered "small group" instruction. For classroom teachers, experience with small group instruction varies widely. Some of us teach reading in a small group format and learn to create and manage the centers that are going on while we're leading one of the small groups. Management can be difficult at times, especially if you have a goal of maximizing the time for all the children so that all their experiences are good learning ones. The age-old problem is how to not have three of your centers be social hour or goof off time!

FOLLOW-UP ACTIVITIES & CENTERS

 In Lessons 1-20, you will find a section called Follow-Up identified by the symbol on the left. These activities can be done whole group, but are also great for placing the children into identical centers with the purpose of getting them ready for independent, unique learning centers. Suggested centers during the first 20 lessons include: 1] Follow-up activity, 2] blocks, 3] housekeeping, 4] meet with teacher to practice the skill from the lesson. Spending 15 minutes in each center with a great plan for rotating would allow a teacher to have a bit of time with a small group of children to reinforce the lesson, evaluate individual children's progress, and do formal or informal assessments.

Starting in Lesson 20, centers and their activities are provided for you, with resources supplied for the centers. Alternate centers are suggested as well.

SUPPLIES AND MATERIALS NEEDED

 Several materials and supplies are used in every lesson. Materials specific to each lesson are detailed in the section called Materials with the symbol shown at left.

For whole group instruction, which is how every lesson begins, the following is what is needed:

TEACHER SUPPLIES
1] Rug on which to gather the children
2] Easel with whiteboard for the teacher
3] Dry erase markers in two colors
4] Small pocket chart
5] Materials supplied in each section of this Manual

STUDENT SUPPLIES
1] Individual whiteboards
2] Marker and tube sock

For Follow-Up and Centers, here is what is needed:

TEACHER SUPPLIES
1] Timer
2] Four centers clearly identified
3] Materials for each center

STUDENT SUPPLIES
1] Personal composition book OR folder filled with appropriately lined paper for journaling. The paper with a blank top is great for this purpose.
2] Inside voices and ears ready to listen!

8

HOW-TO'S

How To Introduce a New Set of Sight Words

 Do this before each new set of words. Gather the children near you and the chart of sight words. This should be an informal introduction time. Prompt discussion and interaction by asking questions like, "Which word do you like best?" "Why do you like that word best?" For specific words, you might comment as follows:

SEE - "What do you think the child sees?"
HELP - "Why is he yelling for help? Do you think he cannot swim? Or is there something in the water?"
DO - "What do you think they are doing in this picture?" (having a picnic)
ON - "What do you have on your table at home?"

Next, you could take a few minutes to let children take turns pointing out a word they recognize. Not a teaching time, remember, just an informal introduction. Once the children have heard each of the words, they will be able to talk about them together and learning will be rapid.

How To Reinforce Learning with Body Motions

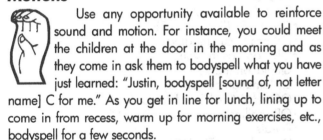 Use any opportunity available to reinforce sound and motion. For instance, you could meet the children at the door in the morning and as they come in ask them to bodyspell what you have just learned: "Justin, bodyspell [sound of, not letter name] C for me." As you get in line for lunch, lining up to come in from recess, warm up for morning exercises, etc., bodyspell for a few seconds.

When the children are well introduced to bodyspelling, you can move into asking them to spell words: "Suzanna, bodyspell CAT for me." As the child bodyspells, she should ALWAYS say the accompanying sounds (not letter names).

How To Utilize Whiteboards in Daily Lessons by Playing Quick Draw

A valuable and integral part of this curriculum is the daily and proper use of whiteboards and markers. I found this practice to be some of the most valuable time spent in terms of student learning.
Each student has her own whiteboard, marker, and tube sock. The marker is stored in the tube sock, and the sock is used for erasing the board quickly during the lesson. Following is the routine you should set up in your classroom:

Bring your lesson materials to the rug. Introduce the new concept (ex: blending "at" words). Model on your whiteboard a couple of examples, then tell the children they will practice sounding and writing next. I call this game Quick Draw. Here is how to play.

Teacher says: Ready? (all eyes must be on you)
Teacher holds up three fingers to represent the three sounds and says: The word is CAT. *(figure 3 on page 10).*
Teacher says: Sound it with me.
All sound: C - A - T. (sounds, not letter names, and teacher is pointing to each finger as she says each sound, showing sound/finger correspondence)
Teacher says: Sound and write.
All sound: C - A - T, with children writing each letter as they say its sound. *It is critical that children sound exactly when they write, as this simple but powerful action is combining all their modalities in the process of learning. Many children will try and just write the letters, or will not want to wait for you to say "sound and write" but you should insist that they play the game correctly. Invariably when a child spells a word incorrectly, leaves off a letter, or mixes up the order of the letters, the simple fix is to have him do the exercise again, this time sounding each sound precisely as they write each letter. I expect even middle schoolers to follow this practice. If the child leaves out the middle letter, point to your fingers again while saying each sound.*
Teacher says: show me your boards.
Children lift boards... corrections made if necessary by re-sounding, not by calling letter names.
Teacher says: Ready? (children look at her).
Teacher repeats the exercise with the new word. An added step could be to quickly bodyspell the word just prior to sounding & writing.

Rules I found essential for the success of this activity:

•absolutely no marks on the whiteboard that are not directed by the teacher (no drawing or scribbling).

•the game is called Quick because we are all listening and quickly following the directions. Eyes on teacher, start when she says write, sound every time you write, etc. Keep game moving.

•when a child did not want to follow directions, she was given the opportunity to use a pencil and paper placed on the whiteboard for that day. She was expected to do the same exercises as the others.

How To Utilize Fingermapping as a Framework for Sound/ Symbol Correspondence

Fingermapping is an exciting and very effective practice that helps beginners or challenged readers actually see the sequence of the sounds they are hearing. Many new and struggling readers reverse, insert, or omit sounds.

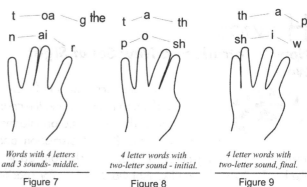

Words with 4 letters and 3 sounds- middle.
Figure 7

4 letter words with two-letter sound - initial.
Figure 8

4 letter words with two-letter sound, final.
Figure 9

Fingermapping prevents all this by providing students with a visual map for each word. Many students simply cannot write new words correctly until they see the fingermap. One look at the map, and they can correctly sound and write the word. For highly visual learners, hearing the sounds is an auditory process, writing is kinesthetic or tactile, but seeing the word mapped out on fingers is a visual clue as to the structure of the word. Over time, the reliance on a visual fingermap diminishes totally, but in the beginning, for some children, the visual structure is the only means by which they can correctly sequence sounds and letters. Using fingermapping is very much like building a bridge over a gap in the road; a gap that would otherwise result in a halt in progress towards reading success.

Figure 1

For words containing up to five letters, the teacher will use the left hand, held up with palm facing the students (figure 1). From this point on, the thumb finger is finger #1/sound #1, the pointer finger is is finger #2/sound #2, tall man finger is finger #3/sound #3, etc. Please note that in order for the sounds to appear in correct sequence for the children sitting in front of you, they will appear backwards to you. This will feel awkward at first, but persist because it will become second nature to you!

In a word with three letters and three sounds like CAT, you will hold up three fingers (figure 2). The fingers are spread apart to show that there are three distinct sounds.

Figure 3 demonstrates the placement of the sounds/letters in the word CAT from your point of view. When you are playing Quick Draw and you are sounding out the word CAT, you will point to the corresponding finger as you sound.

Figure 2

Words with four distinct sounds and letters will be represented as shown in figure 4. The examples shown are the words STOP, and FLAG.

Figure 5 shows the same thing for five letter words with 5 distinct sounds.

The only time you let fingers touch is when you have a four-letter word, but only three sounds such as in PLAY and STAY. (figure 6). Figure 7 shows how you would finger-map words when the two-letter sound spelling is in the center of the word. Figure 9 shows a two-letter final sound.

Words with 3 letters and 3 sounds.
Figure 3

How To Facilitate the Learning of Sight Words

I would strongly recommend using *Activities for Use with SnapWords®* found in Appendix A for a daily warm up with the sight words currently displayed in the pocket chart (one section at a time). The sight words are taught specifically in

Words with 4 letters and 4 sounds.
Figure 4

Words with 5 letters and 5 sounds.
Figure 5

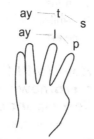
Words with 4 letters and 3 sounds - final.
Figure 6

lessons that follow, but much more is gained by doing the activities in the booklet. The children learn much faster this way rather than when we parcel out one word at a time.

Once a group of sight words is known by all the children, those words can be transferred to the classroom word wall and the next group of stylized sight words put into the pocket chart.

Additional Skills Taught in EFM

- Capitalization - proper and common nouns
- OW, OU /ow/ and OW /oh/
- S /zz/
- Final double L
- Final Y /e/ and /i/
- "Pinchy E" (final silent E)
- Pictures to cue reading
- OU /oo/ as in "you"
- Quotation marks
- Exclamation points
- OO as in "look" and "moon"
- OR spelling pattern as in "porch"
- Plurals
- Digraphs SH, TH, WH, CH
- Final ERE as in "here"
- A /ah/ as in "want"
- Final S as in "likes"
- ABC order
- Past tense
- ING
- Final CK
- R controlled ("Bossy R") sound spellings
- Apostrophe for possession
- Rhyming
- Initial Schwa sound as in "above"
- Compound words
- AY as in "play"
- Long O as in "go"
- Long E as in "he"
- Syllables

Table of Contents:

means display next group of sight words

Section One Goals - Lessons 1-30

LEARNER GOALS:

•The child will enjoy learning that letters are photos of sounds (sound/symbol connection).

•The child will represent each sound in writing and with hand motion.

•The child will acquire the skills of blending and segmenting.

•The child will begin to use knowledge of patterns in spelling for decoding.

•The child will use visuals and motions in recognizing words on sight.

•The child will begin to develop the art of hearing sounds, correlating and representing each sound with the appropriate symbol.

•The child will successfully read and re-read seven books.

MATERIALS NEEDED FOR SECTION 1:

•*Alphabet Tales*
•Alphabet Teaching Cards A, T, C, F, S, P, O, M
•SnapWords® Cards for:

A	
AT	IT
ON	SIT
BY	TO
IN	UP
ME	OR
NO	DO
NOT	HE
THE	HELP
AND	I
GO	MY
IS	SEE

(List A, Groups 1-2)

•Easy-for-Me™ Books, numbers 1-7
  A Cat
  Sap on a Cap
  Tot in a Cot
  Fat Cat
  Pat and Matt
  A Mat on a Tot
  My Cat
•Resources for Section 1: pages 43-106
•Journals: Pronged notebooks with appropriately lined paper for children to use for personal journaling. Journaling will begin in section one and will continue throughout the other sections. Consider using lined paper that has a blank space at the top of the page so children will have a place for illustrating their writing.
•Center Folders: Each child will need a pocket folder with paper in it in which they will record their work during independent centers. I reviewed work as kids came to me for teacher center. Every couple of weeks they got a new supply of paper.
•Whiteboards, markers, and tube socks for each child. I bought a showerboard at Lowes and the salesman cut it into pieces for me so that each child could have a very low cost dry erase board. I assigned a number to each student

and wrote it on their whiteboard, sock and marker so that if there was a mix-up, the belongings could quickly be sorted out. Store personal markers in the tube socks and use them as erasers for the whiteboards. When socks get inky, throw them in the washing machine with bleach and they will get pretty clean! See instructions for playing Quick Draw before this section.

ROOM SET-UP/PREP WORK:

Display the sight words in a pocket chart close enough to the children's eye level that they will be able to gather near the words as they move about the room.

Display the Alphabet in ABC order on the walls.

Prepare all resources you will need for Section 1 and have them accessible for easy retrieval on the day you will use them. I had my students keep their whiteboards in their desks and when we went to the rug, they knew what to bring with them.

Photocopy the Skills Tracking form found in Section 1 Resources, one copy per child. Keep these forms in a file or on a clipboard and update regularly. The beauty of this form is that you may photocopy it from time to time and use it as a means of communicating to parents on the progress of their child.

WORD LISTS for SECTION 1:
(Use these words for segmenting and blending, for pull-down letters, for mixed up words. See individual lessons.)

Sam	fat	mat	pop	pat	pot	sop
mom	moss	sat	cat	cap	map	sap
mop	tap	cot	toss	tot	Tom	caps
mast	fast	past	soft	mats	saps	pats

ASSESSMENTS:

Section 1 is the most critical section in the entire sequence of lessons. It is in this group of 30 lessons that children will learn how to decode and blend. They will also learn their first groups of sight words. It is critical to focus less on how many sounds a child knows as on his facility with blending, decoding, sound substitution, rhyming, and writing the sounds he hears.

If you finish Section 1 and you feel the class is reasonably solid in the skills mentioned above, do some review games, but then go right on into Section 2. If you feel your class could benefit from additional support in the skills listed, take a week or two to do additional activities from Section 1 so that you start Section 2 solidly prepared. Don't assume that some children just won't get it. All the children can succeed, but some might need to always bodyspell, some might rely heavily on visuals to recall their symbols, but as long as every child has something from which to draw, they will be fine! For those children who are struggling a lot, schedule time with them weekly to give them more practice.

The critical question to answer before going on to Section 2 is this: Can my children do the skills that are detailed on the Skills Tracking sheet? These skills are what reading means, so time must be set aside to make sure those skills are in place before going on. Once the children know how to read, they will very quickly pick up the rest of the words and sounds.

1 𝖎📢👂 Aa 👁 a

OBJECTIVES
1. Child will gain a mental visual of A
2. Child will use this visual to recall A
3. Child will connect the visual to the sound
4. Child will utilize the visual in writing A

MATERIALS

1. *Alphabet Tales*, page 7
2. Alphabet Teaching card for Aa
3. SnapWords® card for A
4. Items beginning with short A sound
5. Resources 1-3 (pp. 46-48)
6. Book about ants and their anthills, such as *Ant Cities* by Arthur Dorros (Reading Rainbow book) or Barron's *The Fascinating World of Ants*
7. Better yet, a little trip outside to see an anthill.

1 ANTICIPATORY SET

Use your book about ants, or your little trip outside to see the anthill to spark a little discussion about ants and how they live in tunnels underground. The children would probably like to share experiences they have had with ants. Talk about how the shape of an anthill can be made with their own two hands, fingertips together.

2 STORY

Find the story for A on page 7 of *Alphabet Tales* and read for enjoyment. While you read, slightly emphasize the sounds of short A in the words you read, such as in Alexander and Abigail.

3 VISUAL IMPRINTING

If you begin the practice very early of purposefully storing images in memory, children will begin to rely more and more heavily on the their visual capacities to remember and less on their ability to just copy something they see in front of them.

Ask the children to close their eyes and imagine seeing the anthill with the ants on it. What do they see? Some children will blurt out "It's dark in here!" but others will be able to tell you what they "see" in their mind. The purpose is to use visual imprinting as a means for recalling the shape of the letter A.

4 SIGHT WORD: A

Use the SnapWords® card for A and talk about the girls you see in the visual. The girl in front has A DOLL, meaning only one doll. Let the children tell you what they have: "I have A dog." Emphasize that when A is by itself, it means "one." Review use daily as needed.

5 BODYSPELLING *Alphabet teaching Cards*

Do the motion for A together as you say the short sound of A (like the sound in cat or in ant).

uppercase A   lowercase A

(In the beginning use uppercase exclusively to avoid confusion.)

7 WRITING *Use Handwriting Without Tears*

Spend a few minutes on writing while the children are still gathered in front of you on the rug, or sitting by you if you are teaching one child. As you say the sound together aloud, the child(ren) will practice forming the letter on their whiteboards. If they have difficulty, talk them through the exercise: "Start on the ground, and climb to the top of the hill (**make a slide going up and away from you), then sit on the ground on your bottom and slide down the other side (make a slide going down and away from you.) Next, make a tunnel straight through." Please refer to the back of the Alphabet card for helps with letter formation. In this lesson we are primarily dealing with uppercase A.

Let children write A in their journals and then draw a picture of something. Ex: "A [picture of tree]." Wow! They have written their first phrase!

6 FOLLOW-UP *Resources p. 46-48*

Share the items you collected that begin with short A or use R1*, p 46. Say the names of the items and emphasize the initial short A sound. Then, give the child(ren) a sheet of paper and coloring materials. Let them draw their own anthills as they remember them from the story, and embellish them with all the ants. If you have time for a more involved project, let the children draw one large A and then brush glue with a Q-tip down the two sides and sprinkle sand on the glue. After the glue is dry, they may draw all their ants on their anthill! Great outside project! Allow for share time.

ACROSS THE CURRICULUM

• Science - learn about the habits of ants. Anatomy of the ant: three part body, # of legs & placement, antennae. (see R3)*

• Math - use ants for counting and place them in patterns to practice instant recognition of "how many" ants there are. The goal is to see visually how many rather than rote counting up. (see R2)*

*Please refer to Section 1 resources. (R1) means Resource 1.

**Please refer to writing instructions in the pack of Alphabet Teaching Cards or in the booklet *Writing the Visual, Kinesthetic, & Auditory Alphabet*.

2 ·)))   Tt

OBJECTIVES
1. Child will gain a mental visual of T
2. Child will use this visual to recall T
3. Child will connect the visual to the sound
4. Child will utilize the visual in writing T

MATERIALS

1. *Alphabet Tales*, page 11
2. Alphabet Teaching Card for Tt
3. Objects or pictures of objects that begin with short T sound: (taco, turnip, trowel, tube sock, triangle, tater tots, tomato, tangerine, turtle, tiger, telephone, train, teddybear, turkey, Twizzlers...)
4. Cut out pictures of different types of tables from magazines, hopefully finding one table with a pedestal.
5. Resources 4-6 (pp. 49-51)

ANTICIPATORY SET

Explore your table pictures together. Let the children comment on what they see. Talk about what the various tables are used for. Notice their characteristics (how many legs, the shapes they are, the objects sitting on the tables, etc.). Ask them what they would like to put on their dining table to eat.

STORY

Review the story of A, letting the children tell you what happened in the story. Tell them that you have a new story today that is about Abner and Alexander. Read the story for enjoyment. While you read, slightly emphasize the sound of T in the words you read.

VISUAL IMPRINTING

Ask the children to close their eyes and imagine seeing Abner's table in their heads. What does it look like? What was on the table?

BODYSPELLING

Do the motion for T together as you say the sound of T (do NOT say "tuh", which is two sounds - the T sound and the short U sound).

uppercase T   lowercase T

Next, review together the bodyspelling for A, then T again. Tell the children you are going to play a game in which you say a sound which they will bodyspell. They are not going to know which one you will say, so they will have to listen carefully! Alternate between sounds of A and T.

WRITING

Spend a few minutes sounding and writing T. As you say the sound together aloud, the child(ren) will bodyspell, then practice forming the letter on their whiteboards.

Uppercase T: "Make a thin man by putting your pencil at the top and drawing the line straight down to the floor. Start to one side of his head and draw a nice flat table on top."

Lowercase T: Make a thin man, and then make a table across his shoulders." Talk about how the table needs to be really flat so nothing will roll off!

FOLLOW-UP

Next, share the objects that begin with T. Then share R4. Sort items by kind. Ex: foods, animals, things. Ask them which of the items they would put on their tables to eat.

Give the children their journals and have them draw a nice big T and then load their table with their favorite foods to eat! If they want to draw themselves at the table, that would be great. Allow for sharing time.

ACROSS THE CURRICULUM
• Science - Classify foods and animals. Discuss foods that are good for you vs. foods that are junk and fillers (ex: tomatoes and turkey rather than Twizzlers or Twinkies). Talk about food being our body fuel. (R6)
• Math - teach geometric shapes square, triangle, oval, and circle showing tables with those shapes for tops. Use attribute blocks to practice sorting the shapes by color, by size, or by shape. (R5)
• Health - Teach or review table manners, including washing hands, chewing with your mouth closed, saying please and thank you when asking that food be passed, etc.

LOOKING AHEAD
Our next lesson will blend A and T to make our first word! The skill of blending can be very difficult for some children. Prepare for this by making sure every child is solid in the sound, bodyspelling and shapes of A and T. Bodyspell and sound every chance you get during what would otherwise be wasted time.

Incorporate the following simple exercise into daily morning activities in order to teach and reinforce auditory discrimination, blending and segmenting.

BLEND: Say three sounds and ask the children to guess the word you are sounding: C-A-T,   T-A-P,   T-O-P,   M-O-P,   S-A-T,   T-O-M. Leave a short space between sounds. Increase the length of the words as children gain fluency in this skill.

SEGMENT: This time, start by saying the word, and then break each into individual sounds. Say the word, hold up three fingers to represent the sounds, and point to each finger as you say each sound together.

3  a-t  at

OBJECTIVES
1. Child will review sounds, shapes of A and T
2. Child will blend the two sounds
3. Child will connect the visual of AT to the word
4. Child will sound and write AT

MATERIALS

1. SnapWords® Card for AT
2. Alphabet Teaching Cards for Aa & Tt
3. Plain letter cards for Aa and Tt (p. 59)
4. Snapshots of you at various places
5. Resources 7-8 (pp. 53-54)

ANTicipatory SET

Explore your pictures together, sharing with the children where you were in each photo. Ask them to share their favorite places to be, and why they like being there. Ex: "I like to be at the park so I can swing."

LESSON - Blend AT/Sight Word AT

Review the sounds of A and T, then draw attention to the Alphabet Teaching Cards for those sounds. Say them together again. Next, draw attention to the plain letter cards, showing that the sounds are the same when we read those cards.

Next, ask the children to sound with you as you point to A and then rapidly after, to T. Keep doing this while you move the cards closer and closer together. Finally, sustain the sound of A and add the sound for T on the end, without letting your voice break. Ask the children if they know what word you are saying.

Share the sight word AT, talking about how the same letters in the Alphabet cards are found inside the little house. Say, "The word is at home!" Have the children bodyspell AT, making the shapes of A and T quickly.

VISUAL IMPRINTING

Ask the children to close their eyes and imagine seeing the sight word for AT. Ask them what they "see" inside the little house.

WRITING

Spend a few minutes sounding and writing AT while the children are still near you. First sound AT together while the children bodyspell, then sound AT while the children write each sound.

FOLLOW-UP

While the children are still with you, share that they are going to draw themselves AT their favorite place. Ask a few of the children where they will be in their picture to get the ideas flowing. Supply the children with blank paper and drawing materials and let them create their

page. These pages would make a wonderful classroom book!

The children should start a clean page in their journal for the AT family of words. Today, just write AT at the top.

If desired, do a scavenger hunt in children's books for the word AT. Or the children could hunt through magazines or newspapers for the word AT. They could cut out the word and make a class poster of the ATs they found. If you draw a house on the poster, the children could glue their word inside the house to mimic the SnapWords® Card AT. (R7).

An auditory game that takes no preparation and no materials is as follows. Tell the children they are detectives who listen for clues. They are to give you the silent thumbs up when they hear the sound you tell them you are going to say.

① First have them listen for T words. If they hear you say a word that starts with t-t-t, they are to do the silent thumbs up. Here are some words to use: top, Tim, Sam, trip, map, tap, mom, Tom.

② Next, listen for words that begin with short A. Here are some words to use: apple, ball, ant, alligator, boy, cow, animal, antelope, tiger, balloon, Andrew. A vowel is a harder sound to pick up on, so be sure and enunciate well and even draw out the A slightly when you say the words. Use R8 for follow-up or homework, if desired.

ACROSS THE CURRICULUM

• Geography - Using the idea of being "at home," share with children the homes of children across the world. "At home" looks different for each child! Even within our United States, homes look different from each other. Tie in stories of children in the USA with the map of the United States, to show the children where they live.

• Math - Use upper and lowercase A and T and have the children make up a pattern. An ABABAB pattern could be made in a variety of ways:
A T A T A T   or   A a A a A a   or   T t T t T t.
An AABBAABB pattern could be made like this:
AT at AT at AT at   or   AATTAATT or AAaaAAaa.   Let the children come up with their own patterns.

• Health - Talk about the different ways we act depending on where we are. For instance, when in a store, we stay with the adult we are with, and we don't pull things off the racks. In a restaurant, we use our best table manners, and we use our inside voices so other people can enjoy their meal. In school, we follow directions and respect property and other people. On the playground, we can run and be loud!

ASSESSMENT   Friday

Use the Skills Tracking form and take a few seconds to assess each child individually. Show him/her three things: plain letter cards for A and T, and reverse side of the SnapWord™ card AT. If he can say the sounds and read the word, check off those skills. If a child has difficulty recalling a sound, prompt him to bodyspell. If that doesn't produce the desired result, ask him what the letter looks like. If he is stuck on AT, ask what the word was that we found inside the little house. Avoid just telling the child the answer. Children learn the most if they have to pull up the answer themselves. The motion and /or visual will act as little hooks that reach into their memory and pull out the information.

4 Ff

MATERIALS

1. *Alphabet Tales*, page 15
2. Alphabet Teaching Card for Ff
3. Pictures of flags of all kinds
4. Items that begin with F (R9 p. 55)
5. Resources 10-12 (pp. 56-59)

ANTICIPATORY SET

Explore your flag pictures together. Share with the class that countries and states have flags and that the pictures on the flags have meaning. They show what is important to that country. Our states have flags that have state birds, or flowers, and usually the colors on a flag mean something special to the people of the state or country.

STORY

Read the story for Ff, emphasizing the ffff sound when it occurs.

VISUAL IMPRINTING

Ask the children to close their eyes and imagine seeing the flags on the hill. What can they "see" in their imaginations?

BODYSPELLING

Do the motion for F together as you say the sound for Ffff. Do not say FUH, as this is a combination of the sounds of F and U. All you should hear in the room is the soft sound of air blowing through teeth and lips!

uppercase F   lowercase f

Next, review together the bodyspelling for A, then T. Tell the children you are going to play a game in which you say a sound and they bodyspell it. They are not going to know which one you will say, so they will have to listen carefully! Alternate sounding A, T, and F as they bodyspell. Also have them bodyspell AT.

WRITING

Spend a few minutes saying the sound of F while the children bodyspell, then practice forming the letter on their whiteboards.

Uppercase F: "Make a thin man for the flagpole. Put your pencil on the top of the thin man's head. Make a table. Put your pencil on the thin man's belly button and make one more table."

Lowercase F: "Start on the top line, but instead of making a cave, just start a cave, and then draw the line straight down to the ground. Make a table right through the belly button."

AUDITORY PRACTICE

Blend:

Say three sounds and ask the children to guess the word you are saying: F-O-G, F-I-T, F-A-T, F-A-N, F-U-N.

Segment:

This time, start with the whole word and then break each into their individual sounds. Say the word, hold up three fingers to represent the three sounds, and point to each finger as you say each sound together.

FOLLOW-UP

Share the Objects for F (R9). Is there a way to sort these items? Add these to your class dictionary if you are making one.

Talk with the children about what they would put on a flag if they made one for themselves. What is most important to them? What colors would they use and why? After "priming the pump" to stimulate creativity, have the children use their journals to write a large F and decorate as a flag. (See reverse of Alphabet Card).

If you would like, offer white paper and make the F's into flags. Attach the finished flags to straws, chopsticks, little dowels, or even pipecleaners, if the flags are small enough. The flags would make a cute bulletin board or a refrigerator magnet at home.

ACROSS THE CURRICULUM

• Geography - Link the flags of states to the US map, or country flags to the map of the world.

• Math - reinforce number sequence by making little flags with numbers on them and having the children order them in the correct sequence. (R10)

Discuss the attributes of the flag collection you have. What is alike about the flags? What makes them different from each other? How can you group them? By color? What is the color they see most often? (R11)

MORE!

If you feel there are children who need more practice, take them aside and do this flag activity with them: Take small post-it notes and print the three letters on them you have learned so far. A, T, and F. Have enough for each child. They will put the post-its on the table in front of them. They are to reach for the sound they hear you say. If you say A (short A), they will pick up the picture of that sound and stick it to the table in front of them, etc. Ask, finally, that they choose the two flags they will need to make AT. If they choose the wrong flag, ask them to listen to AT again. Do they hear ffff when you say AT? If necessary, say AT and have the children bodyspell THEN find the flags. (See also R12).

5 f-a-t

MATERIALS

1. SnapWords® Cards for A and AT
2. Alphabet Cards for Aa, Tt, Ff
3. Plain letter cards for Aa, Tt, & Ff
4. Pictures of things that are fat, and that are thin cut from magazines.
5. Resources 13-14 (pp. 60-61)

ANTICIPATORY SET

Explore your pictures together, talking about items that are fat vs. items that are skinny.

LESSON - Blend FAT

Review the sounds for A, T, and F and bodyspell. Review the SnapWord™ AT. Display the plain (reverse side of card) AT, asking the children what it says. Then say, "What would happen if we put this in front of the word AT (moving the plain letter F to the left of the word AT. Sound together, first saying a sustained ffff sound, then finishing with AT. Continue doing this until the sounds are blended together. See if the children can say the word you are blending. If you do not allow your voice to stop between the fff and the AT, the word will be more clear.

Share R14 and discuss what the animals look like. Sort animals into two groups: fat and skinny.

VISUAL IMPRINTING

Ask the children to close their eyes and imagine seeing the sight word FAT. Ask them what they "see" in their imagination. What do you see first? Next? Last? They could bodyspell as they are saying the sounds they "see" in their minds.

WRITING

Spend a few minutes sounding and writing FAT. As you say the sounds together aloud, the child(ren) will bodyspell, then practice writing the word on their whiteboards. Next, ask them to write: "A fat." Show them the sight word for A if they need to review it. Ask them to tell you orally what they will enjoy drawing that is fat to complete their sentence. They will do this during Follow-Up time.

Play the auditory game as before. Tell the children they are detectives who listen for clues. They are to give you the silent thumbs up when they hear the sound you tell them you are going to say.

First have them listen for T words. If they hear you say a word that starts with t-t-t, they are to do the silent thumbs up. Here are some words to use: top, Tim, Sam, trip, map, tap, mom, Tom.

Next, listen for words that begin with short A. Here are some words to use: apple, ball, ant, alligator, boy, cow, animal, antelope, tiger, balloon, Andrew. A vowel is a harder sound to pick up on, so be sure and enunciate well and even draw out the A slightly when you say the words.

Finally, listen for Ff words: fan, house, tree, free, fine, Frank, Mary, door, fit, fall, ant, foot.
(see also R13 for follow-up or homework)

Ask the children to bodyspell what they hear you say:
AT
FAT
AF
FAT
AFT
TAF
TA
FAF
TAT

Use the same words and nonsense words for blending and segmenting practice.

FOLLOW-UP

Supply the children with blank paper and drawing materials and let them create a sentence that says "A fat [draw a picture of something fat]." Again, these pages would make a wonderful class book. Or make a bulletin board with them first, then make the class book once you have taken down the board.

Record FAT in their journal on the AT family page.

ACROSS THE CURRICULUM

• Health - Talk about the need to eat right in order to keep from being overweight. Brainstorm the foods that are good for you and keep you healthy vs. the snacks that are not good for body fuel and make you overweight. (R6)

• Math - Use pictures of fat and skinny things and have the children make up a pattern.

Use the pictures to make addition problems such as: 3 fat cats were sitting on the rug. In came 1 skinny lizard. How many animals are on the rug now?

ASSESSMENT

Do assessments for Ff and add to the S.T. form. Do a second check of the sounds Aa and Tt and the word AT. Give additional help where needed.

6 Cc

OBJECTIVES
1. Child will gain a mental visual of C
2. Child will use this visual to recall C
3. Child will connect the visual to the sound
4. Child will utilize the visual in writing C

MATERIALS

1. *Alphabet Tales*, page 19
2. Alphabet Teaching Card for Cc
3. Book about caves from the library, preferably one also showing animals that live in caves.
4. Pictures of C objects (R15, p. 62)

ANTICIPATORY SET

Share your cave book with the class. Try to create a mood by talking about how dark it is in the cave (like being in a closet with the lights off), and that sometimes it might be damp. There are no plants there because plants need sun and water to grow. Talk about the animals that live in a cave. Obvious choices are bats and bears.

STORY

Read the story for Cc, emphasizing the hard C sound when it occurs, such as in the word CAVE.

VISUAL IMPRINTING

Ask the children to close their eyes and imagine seeing the caves. What did they look like? What was around them? Did they look soft or hard?

BODYSPELLING

Do the motion for C together as you say the sound for ccc. Do not say KUH. All you should hear is the sharp sound of ccc.

Motion for C

Next, review together the bodyspelling for A, T, then F. Tell the children you are going to play a game in which you say a sound and they bodyspell it. They are not going to know which one you will say, so they will have to listen carefully! Alternate sounding A, T, F, and C as they bodyspell. Also have them bodyspell AT, FAT.

WRITING

Spend a few minutes practicing sounding and writing C. As you say the sound together aloud, the child(ren) will bodyspell, then practice forming the letter on their whiteboards.

Uppercase C: "Put your pencil near the top line. Curve around and make a cave."

It is very difficult for children to correctly write the C. They write what looks like a tipsy U. To help with this, have right handed children make a cave with their left hands and draw the C inside this cave. Lefties will stick out their right pointer finger (pretend it is a bear) and draw the cave around the bear!

AUDITORY PRACTICE

Blend:
Say three sounds and ask the children to guess the word you are saying: C-O-G, C-A-T, C-O-T, A-C-T, T-A-C.
Segment:
Use the same words in a different order, and this time break them into their individual sounds. Say the word, hold up three fingers to represent the three sounds, and point to each finger as you say each sound.

If you feel there are children who need more practice, take the group aside and do the flag activity (see lesson 4) with them using the letters F, A, C, T.
Reinforce blending by calling out nonsense combinations and having the children find and position the flags that make up the combinations of sounds. As always, have the children use all their modalities as often as possible. Saying the sound as they pick up the flag, etc.
Use these combinations:

A-C	A-F
C-A	T-A
F-A	F-A-T
T-A-F	T-A-C
A-C-T	

FOLLOW-UP

Share the objects that begin with C from R 15. Is there a way to sort them? Add these to your class dictionary if you are making one.

Talk with the children about what they would 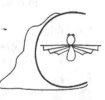 put inside their caves if they had a cave in their backyard. Would it be a bear? A bat family? When they have finished brainstorming, let them draw a huge C in their journals and decorate it like a cave, complete with creatures inside.

ACROSS THE CURRICULUM
• Science - Study what plants need for growth. Animals that live in caves. Hibernation. Nocturnal animals.
Go to www.amazingcaves.com. Download the free teachers guide, which is full of wonderful information on caves.

7  c-a-t

MATERIALS

1. SnapWords® Cards for A and AT
2. Alphabet Teaching Cards for Cc, Ff
3. Plain letter cards for Cc and Ff
4. Pictures of cats and/or a storybook about cats from the library
5. Resource 16 (p.63)

ANTICIPATORY SET

Explore your pictures together, talking about what the animals look like. Which cat do the children like best? Ask how many of them have a cat of their own. Read the story about the cat, if you chose that option.

LESSON - Blend CAT

Review the sounds for A, T, F, C and bodyspell. Display AT, asking the children what it says. Then ask, "What would happen if we put this in front of the word AT?" (as you move the plain letter C to the left of the word AT.) Sound together, first saying the C sound, then finishing with AT. Continue doing this until the sounds are blended together. See if the children can say the word you are blending. If you do not allow your voice to stop between the C and the AT, the word will be more clear. Review F in front of AT.

Put the sight word A by a picture of a cat and "read" with the children. "A Cat." Next, write on your whiteboard or chart paper, "A fat cat" and read it with your children. Underline the AT at the end of FAT and CAT or write those letters with a different color marker, and share with the children that they sound alike at the end because they have the same combination of sounds.

VISUAL IMPRINTING

Ask the children to close their eyes and imagine seeing the word CAT. Ask them what they "see" in their imagination... "What do you see first? Next? Last?" They should bodyspell as they are saying the sounds they "see" in their minds.

WRITING

As you say the sounds C - A - T together aloud, the child(ren) will bodyspell, then practice writing the word on their whiteboards. Next, ask them to write: A CAT making sure they write each sound as they say it outloud. When you have checked whiteboards for accuracy, ask them to write A FAT CAT while they are saying the sound for each letter. Check whiteboards.

AUDITORY PRACTICE

Play the auditory game as before. Children are to give you the silent thumbs up when they hear the sound you are going to say.

Tell them the target sound to listen for, then call out words so they can give you the thumbs up when they hear the correct sound.

Words for T: tap, top, mop, nap, tree, tall, sap
Words for F: fit, nap, fall, follow, apple, nice, fine
Words for A: alligator, ant, card, Abigail, snail, tall, addle, ask
Words for C: cot, cat, map, dot, camp, coat, tot, goat, cap, cast

Sound and Body connection: Ask the children to bodyspell and sound the following:
AC
CAT
CAF
FAC
ACT
TAC
TAF
AFT
AT

Use the same words and nonsense words for blending and segmenting practice.

FOLLOW-UP

Using their journals, ask the children to write their new sentence, A FAT CAT. Your children might love to write "A fat cat at...." and draw their cat someplace really exciting. Again, these pages would make a wonderful class book. Add the word CAT to their journal on the AT page. The children might like to embellish CAT by adding ears and a tail.

ACROSS THE CURRICULUM

• Science - Explore the family of cats... from lions and tigers to house cats. Discuss their similarities and differences. What are the needs of cats in the wild? Where do they get their food? What is their shelter? How do pet cats get their food and shelter? Discuss the difference between wild and domesticated animals. The concept of an animal being endangered could be incorporated into this lesson.
• Math - Use cat pictures (R16) for classification
• Geography - Use the internet or library books to explore the types of cats that are found in various parts of the world. Check out www.bigcats.com.

ASSESSMENT

Do assessments for Cc and add to the S.T. form. Do a second check of the sound Ff and the word FAT. Give additional help where needed.

8   Ss

OBJECTIVES
1. Child will gain a mental visual of S
2. Child will use this visual to recall S
3. Child will connect the visual to the sound
4. Child will utilize the visual in writing S

MATERIALS

1. *Alphabet Tales*, page 23
2. Alphabet Teaching Card for Ss
3. Book about snakes from the library
4. Pictures that start with S (R17)
5. Resources 17-18 (pp. 64-65)

ANTICIPATORY SET

Ask the children if they have ever seen a real snake before. If so, where were they? What did it look like? Were they scared of it or just really curious? Ask them what they know about snakes, then share your book or other materials with them.

STORY

Read the story for Ss, emphasizing the soft hissing Sss sound when Spotty Snake speaks.

VISUAL IMPRINTING

Ask the children to close their eyes and imagine seeing Spotty Snake. What did he look like? Did he look the same at the end of the story as he did at the beginning? If not, how did he change?

BODYSPELLING

Do the motion for S together as you hiss the sound for S.

Motion for S

Next, review together the bodyspelling for A, T, F, C. Have the children bodyspell the sounds they know now, then bodyspell AT, FAT, CAT.

WRITING

As you say the sound for S together aloud, the child(ren) will bodyspell, then practice forming the letter on their whiteboards.

Start to make a cave, then as you get near the bottom, change your mind and make a curve going the other way...right under the cave!

See the illustration of how the children can use their own hand-caves to help them form the shape of their new letter. Lefties would form a cave with their right hands, start with their pencil over their fingers (on top

of their hand-caves) and make the first curve around their fingers, then the bottom curve inside their hand-caves. In other words, the bottom curve of their S will fit inside their hand-cave.

AUDITORY PRACTICE

Blend: Say three sounds and ask the children to guess the word you are saying   C-O-G,   C-A-T,   C-O-T, A-C-T,   T-A-C.

Segment: Use the same words in a different order, and this time break them into their individual sounds. Say the word, hold up three fingers to represent the three sounds, and point to each finger as you say each sound.

Auditory Discrimination: Use R18 for auditory practice, either in school or for homework.

If you feel there are children who need more practice, take the group aside and do the flag activity with them using the letters F, A, C, T, S. (see Lesson 4)

Reinforce blending by calling out nonsense combinations and having the children find and position the flags that make up the combinations of sounds. As always, have the children use all their modalities as often as possible. Say the sound as they pick up the flag, etc.
Use these combinations:

S-A-C	S-A-F
S-A	T-A-S
F-A-S	S-A-T
T-A-F	T-A-C
A-S-T	C-A-S

FOLLOW-UP

Share the objects that begin with S from R 17. Is there a way to sort them? Add these to your class dictionary if you are making one.

Tell the children that they will be making snakes. How are they going to decorate their snakes? Are the snakes going to be spotted like Spotty Snake? Or are they going to be striped? Are they going to make a poisonous snake or a friendly snake?

ACROSS THE CURRICULUM
• Science - Study snakes and how they live, what they eat, etc.

Identify other reptiles. Animals hatched from eggs rather than born live.

 **9** **s-a-t**

OBJECTIVES
1. Child will review sounds A, T, F, C, S
2. Child will blend the sounds for SAT
3. Child will sound and write SAT
4. Child will identify the rhyming parts of words (fat, cat, sat)

MATERIALS

1. SnapWords® Cards for A and AT
2. Alphabet Cards Ss, Cc and Ff
3. Plain letter cards for Ss, Ff, Cc, Aa, Tt (2)
4. Resource 19 (p. 66)

ANTicipatory SET

 Fire up the imaginations of your children by asking "Where is your favorite place to sit?" What do you do when you sit there? What would be the funniest place you can sit? How would you like to sit on a nice wooly sheep? A tall prickly cactus? A bucking horse?

You could play a game called "Hot Seat." You start the game, holding a small beanbag. Say, "I sat on a rug." Toss the beanbag to a child and he will say quickly, "I sat on..." and toss the bean bag to another child.

LESSON - Blend SAT

Display the SnapWord™ AT and ask the children what they think they might put with AT to make the word SAT. What sound do they hear just before they say the word AT? Guide them into hearing the sound Ssssss. Then if they hear it, ask them how they would bodyspell that sound. The nice thing about the sound for S is that it is easy to hear and easy to blend! Get everyone saying Ssssss as you move the S card to the front of AT and then finish the sounds without a break in your voice. SssssAT.

Using the plain alphabet cards, display A and T next to each other. Decode together. Then add the C and ask the children to decode or read that word. Ask, "What would happen if I take off the Ccc and put a Fff in its place?" Decode together. "What would happen if I take off the Fff and put a Ttt in its place?" Decode together.

Put the sight word A by a picture of a cat and "read" with the children. "A cat." Next, write on your whiteboard or chart paper, "A fat cat" and read it with your children. Next, write "A fat cat sat!" Read together, and again, identify the parts of the words that make them rhyme. Write these letters in a different color so they stand out well.

VISUAL IMPRINTING

 Ask the children to close their eyes and imagine seeing the word SAT. Ask them what they "see" in their imagination. "What do you see first? Next? Last?" They should bodyspell as they are saying the sounds they "see" in their minds. "Where does Spotty Snake come in the word? At the first or the middle or on the end?" Ask the

children to write on their whiteboards what they saw in their imaginations.

WRITING

 Spend a few minutes sounding and writing SAT. As you say the sounds together aloud, the child(ren) will bodyspell, then practice writing the word on their whiteboards. Next, ask them to write: A CAT. When you have checked whiteboards for accuracy, ask them to write A FAT CAT while they are saying the sound for each letter. Check whiteboards. Then add the word SAT to the phrase.

AUDITORY PRACTICE

Play the auditory game as before.
Words for T: taps, tip, top, slant, trail, tell, sit
Words for F: flag, sap, fell, fellow, pie, fin, fine
Words for C: cast, cap, tap, dot, clap, Chris, ton, cap.
Words for S: sip, step, mop, clap, soup, silly, sun, fun, boy.
Sound and Body connection: Ask the children to bodyspell and sound the following:
AC
SAT
CAS
FAS
SAC
TAS
SAF
AST

Use the same words and nonsense words for blending and segmenting practice.

FOLLOW-UP

 Before breaking into groups for the follow-up activities, brainstorm with your children where they will draw their cat who sat. Some might want to be funny, while others might be in the mood to create a nice cozy place for their cat to sit.

Ask the children to write their new sentence (A FAT CAT SAT) in their journals, and add the word SAT to the AT family page. They will draw their cat sitting on something. Their drawing could be of them sitting on something and their cat sitting on something else near them.

ACROSS THE CURRICULUM

• Math - Classification, sorting. Use pictures of all sorts of chairs cut from magazines. Discuss how to sort them, whether by use, by size, by texture (hard or soft) etc. Show them ONE chair and ask them how many legs it has. Show them a picture of two chairs and ask how many legs there are now. See who can tell you how many legs on three chairs! See R19 for follow-up or homework.

ASSESSMENT

Do assessments for Ss and add to the S.T. form.

10 Oo

OBJECTIVES
1. Child will gain a mental visual of O
2. Child will use this visual to recall O
3. Child will connect the visual to the sound
4. Child will utilize the visual in writing O

MATERIALS

1. *Alphabet Tales*, page 27
2. Alphabet Teaching Card for Oo
3. Pictures of items that start with O (R20)
4. A safety mirror to pass around
5. Resources 20-23 (pp. 67-70)

ANTICIPATORY SET

Ask the children how many of them have been to the dentist and had their teeth checked. Ask them what the dentist says to them. Does he say, "Open wide?" Say, "What do you think the dentist sees when you open wide?" Pass around the mirror and let the children look at their wide open mouths. Discuss what they see in the mirror. Ask them what shape their mouths are when they are open really wide. (A circle, an O, etc.)

Ask the children, "What are some things that we put in our mouths?" The obvious answer is food. But there are other things we put in our mouths, such as toothbrushes and toothpaste. Talk about things that little tiny children might put in their mouths, like pencils, pens, coins, string to chew on, etc. Have them give you examples of things that are good to put in their mouths, and things that are NOT good!

STORY

Read the story for Oo, emphasizing the O sound by opening your mouth wide (making an O with your wide open mouth.)

VISUAL IMPRINTING

Ask the children to close their eyes and imagine seeing Oscar Ovall when he was crying at the end of the story. What did his mouth look like? They can make the Oscar mouth even with their eyes closed!

BODYSPELLING

Do the motion for O together as you open your mouth very wide and say the O sound (sounds like Ah as in POT).

Motion for O

Next, review together the bodyspelling for newest letters. Have the children bodyspell the sounds they know now, then bodyspell SAT, FAT, CAT.

WRITING

As always, practice sounding and then forming the letter on their whiteboards.

Make a cave, but then close up the mouth of the cave so nothing can come in!

AUDITORY PRACTICE

Blend: Say three sounds and ask the children to guess the word you are saying:
C-O-T,   T-O-T,   P-O-T,   T-O-P.

Segment: Use the same words in a different order, and this time break them into their individual sounds. Say the word, hold up three fingers to represent the three sounds, and point to each finger as you say each sound.

AUDITORY/TACTILE PRACTICE

Use Post-it notes with letters on them, or simply use letter tiles to do this activity: Call out nonsense combinations and have the children find and position the flags or tiles that make up the combinations of sounds. They should say the sound as they pick up the letter. Really active children would probably prefer to use sticky notes, stand up, and stick the letters to the refrigerator, a white board or the wall.

Use these combinations:
S-O-C   S-A-F   S-O-T   T-A-S   F-O-S   S-A-T
T-O-F   T-A-C   O-S-T   C-A-S

FOLLOW-UP

Share the objects that begin with O (R20). Is there a way to sort them? Add these to your class dictionary if you are making one.

Tell the children that they will be drawing Oscar Ovall in their journals, showing his very wide open mouth. They get to choose what to draw

inside Oscar's mouth. It might be olives, okra, or something else like an octopus!!!! OR they might decide that Oscar is crying about something with his mouth wide open and they can decide what he's crying about.

ACROSS THE CURRICULUM

• Math - Counting by 2's. Find 2's of things first. Two socks, shoes, eyes, hands, feet. Find 4's like legs on tables and chairs, legs on a dog, cat, horse, etc. 6's like legs on an ant. 8's like legs on a spider and legs on an OCTOPUS! (R21)

Use pictures of olives for counting, adding, subtracting. (R22-23)
• Science - Study the octopus.
• Health - Dental hygiene.

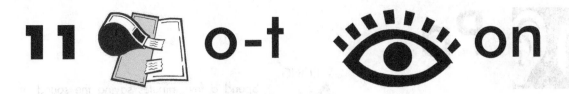 **11** **o-t** **on**

OBJECTIVES

1. Child will review all their sounds
2. Child will use their sounds to blend for OT family of words
3. Child will practice rhyming
4. Child will learn initial sound replacement in forming new words
5. Child will learn the sight word ON

MATERIALS

1. Plain letter cards for A, T, F, C, S, O
2. SnapWords® Card for ON
3. Outline of a toolbox taped to teacher whiteboard (R25, p. 72)
4. Sticky tack or tape; magnetic letters for A, T, F, C, S, O if you would rather not tape pr sticky tack your print ones to the whiteboard.
5. Magazine cutouts of various tools (or R24, p. 71)

ANTICIPATORY SET

The outline of the toolbox (R25) should be the focal point for this part of the lesson. Introduce the idea that when we do a job, we need tools. "If you were going to bake a cake, what tools might you need?" (Bowl, spoon, measuring spoons and cups, etc.) "If you want to build a bird house, what tools might you need?" As you brainstorm, tape or stickytac the pictures of tools you found inside the toolbox (R24).

Say, "Today, we are going to build something and we need tools, too. We are going to build some words, and these will be our tools." While you are talking, remove the tool pictures and post the letters you prepared inside the toolbox.

LESSON - Blending with OT

"If we want to build the word CAT, what tools should we get from our toolbox?" Let the children volunteer to identify the sounds needed from the toolbox. As the correct letter sounds are chosen, write them on the whiteboard.

"If we want to build the word FAT, what tools do we need?" As the correct letters are chosen, write them under CAT on your whiteboard.

Ask, "How are these two words alike?" (at)
Then, "How are they different?" (c and f)
Next do the word SAT and write it under the other two words.

Display the letters O and T. Sound together until the children are blending them into OT.

Say, "What if I put a Ttt on the front of OT? What would we have?" Write TOT and let the children decode.

Say, "What if I take off the T and put a Ccc there instead? What would we have?" Erase the T and write a C in its place. Decode COT together.

VISUAL IMPRINTING

Ask the children to close their eyes and imagine seeing the word TOT. Ask where O is. Beginning, middle or the end? Ask them to write what they saw as soon as they open their eyes.

Spend a few minutes sounding and writing OT, TOT, COT, SOT on their whiteboards.

SIGHT WORD: ON

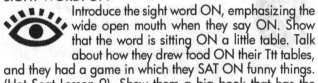

Introduce the sight word ON, emphasizing the wide open mouth when they say ON. Show that the word is sitting ON a little table. Talk about how they drew food ON their Ttt tables, and they had a game in which they SAT ON funny things. (Hot Seat Lesson 9). Show them a big book that has the word ON several times and see if the children can quickly locate the word on the page.

Play a version of Hot Seat, asking the children to say quickly what is ON the table.

WRITING

Practice writing the sight word ON. Play Quick Draw using the OT family words: COT, TOT. Dictate and sound the sentence, A TOT ON A COT. Make sure all students are sounding as they write the letters. Next, dictate and sound, "A fat cat sat on a cot."

Sound and Body connection: Ask the children to bodyspell and sound the following:
OC   SOT   COS   FOS   SOC   TOS   SOF   OST
Use the same words and nonsense words for blending and segmenting practice.

FOLLOW-UP

The children will break into small groups to draw their sentence: "A fat cat sat ON [picture]." They can make up where the cat sat.

The children also will start an OT family page and add the OT words to it that they made today: COT, TOT

ACROSS THE CURRICULUM

• Science - Classification, sorting. Use pictures of all sorts of tools cut from magazines or R24. Sort the tools into groups depending on their use.
• Social Studies - Workers and their tools; tie in the sense of community and how all of us should contribute our talent, work and efforts to our communities. Brainstorm ways in which we can contribute at home, at school, and in our neighborhoods (picking up trash, etc.).

ASSESSMENT

Update S.T. form as needed. It would be best to do two assessments on each skill just to be sure the child really has mastered each one. There is a space on the tracking form to date the assessments.

12 Pp

OBJECTIVES
1. Child will gain a mental visual of Pp
2. Child will use this visual to recall Pp
3. Child will connect the visual to the sound
4. Child will utilize the visual in writing Pp

MATERIALS

1. *Alphabet Tales*, page 31
2. Alphabet Teaching Card for Pp
3. Pictures of items that start with P (R26, p. 73)
4. A safety mirror to pass around
5. Small backpack with camping gear

ANTICIPATORY SET

Ask the children how many of them have spent the night away from home. Let them share their experiences for a few minutes. Then ask what they packed to go overnight. Show them your pack and share with them that if you go camping in the mountains, you pack things you might need for the trip.

STORY

Read the story for Pp, emphasizing the Pp. At the end of the story, pass around a mirror and let the children take turns making the soft puffing sound that is Pppp. (NOT "puh.") If they hold the mirror close to their mouths, they might see the tiny cloudy spot on the mirror from their warm breath.

VISUAL IMPRINTING

Ask the children to close their eyes and imagine seeing Peter and Paul with their packs on their backs. Which way were they walking in the story? (to the left - the children will likely just point and say "over there!")

BODYSPELLING

Do the motion for P together as you say the sound. When you put your left hand up nice and tall, you can say, "Here's Pete" and then when you add the right hand in a cupped shape, say, "... and here's his PACK." Using this language and these motions will help the children keep from reversing the letter P, which is a common problem with young children.

Motion for P

Next, review together the bodyspelling for newest letters. Have the children bodyspell the sounds they know now, then bodyspell SAT, FAT, CAT, COT, TOT.

WRITING
Spend a few minutes saying the sound of Pp while the children are still near you. As you say the sound together aloud, the child(ren) will bodyspell, then practice forming the letter on their whiteboards.

"Make a thin man named Pete or Paul, then add a pack high up on his back."

AUDITORY PRACTICE
Blend: Say three sounds and ask the children to guess what you are saying:
S-A-T, F-A-T, C-A-T, C-O-T, T-O-T.

Segment: Use the same words in a different order, and this time break them into their individual sounds. Say the word, hold up three fingers to represent the three sounds, and point to each finger as you say each sound.

ORAL/TACTILE PRACTICE:
Reinforce blending by calling out nonsense combinations and having the children find and position the flags or tiles that make up the combinations of sounds. They should make the sound as they pick up the letter.

You may use these combinations:
S-O-C   S-A-F   S-O-T   T-A-S   F-O-S   S-A-T
T-O-F   T-A-C   O-S-T   C-A-S

FOLLOW-UP

Share the objects that begin with P (R26). Is there a way to sort them? Add these to your class dictionary if you are making one.

Tell the children that they will be drawing a picture in their journals of Pete and Paul with big packs on their backs. They are to brainstorm and draw what they think the boys need to have in their packs.

If they prefer, they may cut pictures out of magazines, but I personally prefer letting the children draw for themselves as it requires a lot more of their creativity.

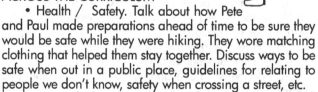

ACROSS THE CURRICULUM
• Health / Safety. Talk about how Pete and Paul made preparations ahead of time to be sure they would be safe while they were hiking. They wore matching clothing that helped them stay together. Discuss ways to be safe when out in a public place, guidelines for relating to people we don't know, safety when crossing a street, etc.

Tie in with the general topic of thinking ahead and being prepared. For instance, just as we gathered tools ahead of time in the last lesson, in this lesson the boys thought ahead and packed what they needed. In our lives the application can be to develop the habit of thinking about what we need to take home from school every day or what we need to do at home to prepare for school the next day.

13 p-a-t

MATERIALS

1. SnapWords® Cards for A, ON and AT
2. Plain letter cards for sounds A, T, F, C, P
3. Student journals
4. Pocket chart for making words
5. Resource 27 (p. 74)

ANTICIPATORY SET

"Did you know that there are two kinds of PATs?" Wait for responses... then add, "One is the kind we do when we pat someone on the back for doing a great job, or when we pat our puppy's head. The other is PAT, the name of a person! Do any of you know someone named Pat?" Write pat and Pat on the whiteboard and review the idea of a name starting with a capital letter. That is how we can tell which kind of pat we are reading: lowercase for the motion of patting, uppercase for the name of a person. Erase the whiteboard.

LESSON - Blend PAT

"Let's figure out what we will need if we build the word PAT." Start with the ending sounds of AT in your pocket chart and ask the children to identify the sound they will need to put with the AT to make PAT.

Then replace the P with a C and ask the children to decode or read that word. Ask, "What would happen if I take off the Ccc and put a Fff in its place?" Decode together. "What would happen if I take off the Fff and put a Ttt in its place?" Decode together.

Put the sight word A by a picture of a cat and "read" with the children "A Cat." Next, write on your whiteboard or chart paper, "A Fat Cat" and read it with your children. Next, write "A Fat Cat Sat!" Read together, and again, identify the parts of the words that make them rhyme. Color them in a different color, underline them or make them visually stand out in some way.

VISUAL IMPRINTING

Ask the children to close their eyes and imagine seeing the word PAT. Ask them what they "see" in their imagination. What do you see first? Next? Last? They could bodyspell as they are saying the sounds they "see" in their minds. Where does Ttt come in the word? At the beginning or the middle or on the end? Ask the children to write on their whiteboards what they saw in their imaginations.

WRITING

Sound and write PAT as you say the sounds together aloud. The child(ren) will bodyspell, then practice writing the word on their whiteboards. Next, ask them to write: A cat. When you have checked whiteboards for accuracy, ask them to write A FAT CAT while they are saying the sound for each letter. Check whiteboards. Then add the word SAT to the phrase. They have more options for sentences now! They can write I PAT A FAT CAT. A FAT CAT SAT ON PAT. They can even write PAT SAT ON A FAT CAT!

AUDITORY PRACTICE

Play the auditory game as before.

Words for T: taps, tip, top, sled, trail, tell, send
Words for F: flag, sap, fell, fellow, pie, fin, fine
Words for C: cast, cap, tap, dot, clap, Chris, ton
Words for S: sip, step, mop, clap, soup, silly, sun
Words for P: pat, fit, top, Pete, Pam, sit, pot, toss

Sound and Body connection: Ask the children to bodyspell and sound the following:

AP
PAT
CAP
FAS
SAC
PAS
SAF
ASP

Use the same words and nonsense words for blending and segmenting practice.

FOLLOW-UP

Before doing the follow-up activities, brainstorm with your children about whether they are going to write and draw about a girl or boy named Pat, or are they going to draw themselves patting an animal. Which will it be? Teacher will circulate among the groups if in school, or will initiate each activity if at home.

ONE: start the follow up activity.
TWO: add PAT to their page of AT words. Children also need to start an OP family page in their journals and add POP, COP, TOP.
THREE: unscramble a sentence (See R27)

ACROSS THE CURRICULUM
• Science - Care of a pet (choose one).

ASSESSMENT
Do assessments for Pp and add to the S.T. form.

14 o-p & o-t

MATERIALS

1. Plain letter cards for A, T, F, C, S, O, P (2)
2. Toolbox outline if desired (R25)
3. Pocket chart if desired
4. Resource 28 (p. 75)

ANTicipatory SET

Place the letter cards in the toolbox OR place them in a row in a pocket chart down where the children can easily see them.

Tell them we have some jobs to do and now we have our tools all ready. Have them put on their thinking caps so that they are all ready.

Say, "Did you know that there are three different ways to use the word POP?" Wait for responses...and let the children try and guess the three ways... then add, "One way we use POP is when our balloon pops! Some people call their dad POP. Some people call soft drinks POP!"

"Which tools will we need if we build the word POP?"

LESSON - Blending with OP and OT

Put the letters for PAT in your pocket chart or write them on your whiteboard. After the children have read PAT, say, "What will happen to PAT if we take off the Ppp and replace it with a Ccc?" Decode the word CAT together.

Change the final T to a P and sound together: CAP. What if we take away the C and put an S there instead? Decode SAP. AP words: CAP, SAP, PAP, TAP. "What do these words have that are alike? AP. These are the AP family words!"

Draw attention to TAP and say, "We are going to take away two of these letters and put a new one up." Take away the P, A and put an O by the T to make OT. "What does this say now?" Continue to make OT words: COT, TOT, POT. Ask, "What is alike about these words? OT." Say "These are OT family words!"

While POT is still displayed, take the T off the end and ask the children what is left. PO___. Add a P on the end and sound the word out together. POP. Continue with OP words: COP, SOP, TOP. "What do these words have that is alike? OP. These are the OP family words!"

VISUAL IMPRINTING

Ask the children to close their eyes and imagine seeing the word POT. Ask where O is. Beginning, middle or the end? Ask them to write what they saw as soon as they open their eyes.

WRITING

Spend a few minutes sounding and writing OT, TOT, COT, SOT, OP, TOP, COP, SOP on their whiteboards.

Sound and Body connection:

Ask the children to bodyspell and sound the following:
OP   POT   POS   FOP   SOP   TOP   SOT   POC
Use the same words and nonsense words for blending and segmenting practice.

FOLLOW-UP

The children will break into small groups to write their sentence and illustrate it in their journals: "A fat cat sat on Pat." Or "A fat cat sat on top." Or "A fat cat sat on Pop."

In another group, children will begin to write families of words in their journals: AT, AP, OP, OT.

In a third group, see R28 for a sheet the children can use to read and illustrate. School at home? Do the activities in sequence with your child.

ACROSS THE CURRICULUM

• Social Studies - Continue study of workers and their tools. Choose specific community helpers to read about. Ideas include anyone who performs a job in the community without which we would be lost! Trash collectors, postal workers, police officers, fire fighters, teachers, doctors, librarians, etc.

• Language Arts - Begin the practice of sequencing events in a story. Do oral sequencing first, using words such as "first, next, and last." Move to a more independent task such as giving the children a sheet of paper with three large squares on it. Ask them to draw something that happened first in the story we last read in *Alphabet Tales*, what happened next, and what happened at the end. Model sequencing yourself each time you finish reading a story.

ASSESSMENT

Update S.T. form as needed.

15  the

OBJECTIVES
1. Child will review sight words A, AT, & ON
2. Child will learn sight word THE
3. Child will find sight words in print
4. Child will use sight words in sentences

MATERIALS

1. SnapWords® Cards for A, AT, ON, THE
2. Plain word wall cards for A, AT, ON & THE (see Appendix B, p. 287)
3. Pocket chart
4. Big book story that has many instances of the four sight words learned to date
5. Resource 29 (p. 76)
6. Small magnifying glasses, if desired

ANTICIPATORY SET

Place the SnapWords® in the pocket chart with the plain word wall words next to them so that SnapWords® A is by plain A, etc.

Open your big book and tell the children they are going to be detectives looking for special clues while you read. (I found at one time some very inexpensive plastic magnifying glasses only two inches long, but great for playing these detective games as each child could have one.) Tell them that they are going to be looking for these words in the story that you read and when they see one of the words, they are going to hold up their magnifying glass (or give the silent thumb up if they don't have glasses).

LESSON - Sight Word THE

Draw attention to the sight words in the chart and review quickly with the children. Introduce THE by saying that this is a word that is used ALL the time! You cannot sound it out! You just have to get used to his face and remember the sounds of the word. The visual that goes with THE is a set of several the's of varying sizes and colors. This is to show that the word appears just everywhere!

Open to the first page of your story and find a THE for the children so they can see what they will be looking for. See if someone can find an A or AT or ON. Then settle in to read the story, while the children watch carefully for their sight words.

VISUAL IMPRINTING

Ask the children to close their eyes and imagine seeing the word THE. What is the shape they see first? Let the children write the word on their whiteboards. This time they will not sound individual sounds! Point out that there is a pattern in the height of the letters: tall, tall, short.

WRITING

Spend a few minutes practicing writing THE. Then ask your children for ideas on how to end the sentence they are starting when they write THE. The what? They already know how to write "The cat." In fact they could make a bit longer of a sentence. I know! Let's play a game where each time you write a sentence, you make it one word longer!

Start with "Cat."
Add a word: "The cat."
Add a word: "The cat sat."
Add a word: "The fat cat sat."
Add a word: "Pat the fat cat sat."
Add two words: "Pat the fat cat sat on Pop."

FOLLOW-UP
The children will write a sentence using as many of the sight words as they can. "The fat cat at [picture]." "The cat on Pat." "I pat the cat." See R29 which also contains a word bank. If at school, break into small groups for this activity.

Add THE to their journals.

If desired, use old newspapers and magazines and let the children look for instances of the word THE which they can cut out and glue on a class poster. It would be fun to see how many different fonts and sizes the children find! Beside each THE, the children could paste pictures of things they found in the magazines.

ACROSS THE CURRICULUM
• Language Arts - Do a sequencing activity where the children make up three places their cat is AT in their story. Maybe the cat decided to go for a walk and went visiting some places in town, or maybe you took your cat with you and took pictures of him sitting in different places.

On a large sheet of paper with three boxes, the children should draw their cat in three places. The boxes are labeled "First", "Next," and "Last." Under each picture the children could write: "The cat at the zoo." etc. Of course, the children will need to generate a word bank with you to use for labeling their pictures. Ask them to give you ideas for the places they want to use, and then write the words for them in a word bank for them to copy when they label their work.

ASSESSMENT
Assess for sight word recognition, adding THE to the S.T. form when you feel the children are able to recognize the word on sight.

16 Mm

MATERIALS

1. *Alphabet Tales*, page 35
2. Alphabet Teaching Card for Mm
3. Pictures of items that start with M (R30, p. 77)
4. A safety mirror to pass around
5. Pictures of mountains, or a story book with good illustrations of mountains

ANTICIPATORY SET

Share with the children your pictures or story of the mountains. Then talk about some of the things you might find in the mountains that might not be found in the flatlands. The vegetation is different, and the animals that are found in the mountains might be very different from what the children are familiar with where they live.

STORY

Read the story for Mm, emphasizing the Mmm sound. If you would like to, pass the mirror around to let the children see the shape of their mouths when they are sounding Mm.

VISUAL IMPRINTING

Ask the children to close their eyes and imagine seeing the mountains they heard about in the story today. How many "humps" did they see in the first set of mountains. Where are the points? If you are going to climb a mountain, would you start in the air or on the ground?

BODYSPELLING

uppercase M　　　　　lowercase M

Do the motion for Mm together and say the sound. Point out the shape of your hands, that the wide part is at the bottom and the pointed part is on the top. Some children have trouble in making an M because they see the zig-zag shape, but are not quite sure where to start writing.... in the air or on the ground!

Next, review together the bodyspelling for newest letters. Have the children bodyspell the sounds they know now, then bodyspell SAT, FAT, CAT, COT, TOT, POT, TOP.

WRITING

Sound Mm together. As you say the sound together aloud, the child(ren) will bodyspell, then practice forming the letter on their whiteboards. "Climb the mountain, then sit down and slide down the other side, and then do it all over again!"

AUDITORY PRACTICE

Blend: Say three sounds and ask the children to guess what you are saying:

S-A-M, F-A-T, P-O-P, C-A-P, M-O-P, M-O-M, C-O-T

Segment: Use the same words in a different order, and this time break them into their individual sounds. Say the word, hold up three fingers to represent the three sounds, and point to each finger as you say each sound.

ORAL/TACTILE PRACTICE

Reinforce blending by calling out nonsense combinations and having the children find and position the flags or tiles that make up the combinations of sounds. They should make the sound as they pick up the letter.

Use these combinations:

S-O-M　M-A-F　S-O-F　M-A-S　F-O-M　S-A-M
M-O-F　T-A-M　O-S-T　　C-A-M

FOLLOW-UP

Share the objects that begin with M (R30). Is there a way to sort them? Add these to your class dictionary if you are making one.

Tell the children that they will be drawing the big mountains that Pete and Paul and the other climbers hiked on. They should draw the mountains very large because they need to have room for making trees, stick men, a river or whatever else they want to make. They could even draw some animals on their mountains!

ACROSS THE CURRICULUM

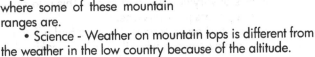

• Geography - Show the children pictures of mountains that are snow-covered, pictures of our well-known mountain ranges. Show them on a map where some of these mountain ranges are.

• Science - Weather on mountain tops is different from the weather in the low country because of the altitude.

17 m-a-t

OBJECTIVES
1. Child will review all their sounds
2. Child will use their sounds to blend MAT
3. Child will review rhyming with AT
4. Child will learn final sound replacement in forming new words

MATERIALS

1. Plain letter cards: A, T, F, C, S, O, P, M
2. Toolbox outline from R25 (p. 72)
3. Resource 31 (p. 78) & R27 (p. 74)

ANTICIPATORY SET

Place the letter cards in the toolbox OR place them in a row in a pocket chart down where the children can easily see them.

We are going to build some new words today, so we have our tools all ready! How many letters do we know now? Let a child count them. We have 8 sounds in our toolbox now!

Say, "I will put these two letters together first (put A and T together). This is so easy!" Sound AT. Ask, "What sound can we put in front of AT to make it say PAT?" "What sound can we put instead of the Pp so that we can make SAT?" Continue in this manner until you have Mm left. Say the sound for Mm first, and then move it closer to the AT and finally combine the sounds to make the word MAT.

LESSON - Blending with M

Continue the lesson by doing sound replacement for T. You have MA displayed. Ask, "What can we put at the end of MA to make the word MAT?" Be sure they know to select the T, then ask, "What can we put after the MA to make the word MAP?" "What letter would we change to make the word CAP?" Repeat with SAP.

Ask, "If I take off the P and put a new letter up here (replace the P with an M) what word will I have now?" (SAM). "What if I take off the S and put a Pp on the front. What word will we have then?" (PAM)

VISUAL IMPRINTING

Ask the children to close their eyes and imagine seeing the word MAT. Ask where Mm is. Beginning, middle or the end? Where is the Tt? Sound MAT together and ask them to write what they saw as soon as they open their eyes.

WRITING

Spend a few minutes sounding and writing all the words they can make now with their eight letters! Among them: Sam, fat, mat, pop, Pat, pot, sop, Mom, sat, cat, cap, map, sap, mop, tap, cot, am, Tom, Matt!

Sound and body connection: Ask the children to bodyspell and sound the following:

MOP POM MOS FOM SOM TOM MOT MOC
PAM SAM TAM CAM

Use the same words and nonsense words for blending and segmenting practice as needed.

FOLLOW-UP

Group one will draw and write their sentence in their journals: "A fat cat sat on a mat." They will also add MAT to the AT family page, and start clean pages for AP and AM families. Include: CAP, MAP, TAP, SAP, SAM, and PAM.

Another group can work together sorting word cards of the words they can decode by putting them into families by ending.

Yet another group may play Bingo or Go Fish with supervision. (R31)

A fourth group can take a cut-apart sentence and put it into the right order, and then glue it onto a fresh sheet of paper. (see R27)

The teacher's role is still to make sure the centers remain on task and focused. Later, centers will have to function independently while you are leading a small group, so this is the goal to keep in mind at this point! Of course, teachers at home will do these activities in sequence with their child.

ACROSS THE CURRICULUM

• Language Arts - Children may begin to distinguish between proper nouns and common nouns. In the group of words they can now decode are a few names. Help them learn to identify the words that are names and begin to write them with an initial capital letter. Their own name should always begin with a capital letter.

Introduce and review by doing an oral game in which you call out words and names. The children are to listen closely and give you the silent thumbs-up when they hear a proper noun (names).

ASSESSMENT

Update S.T. form as needed.

18

MATERIALS

1. Writing materials and paper
2. A giant book with simple language
3. An easel and pad
4. Pocket chart and words on cards
5. Resources 31-35 (pp. 78-82)

ANTICIPATORY SET

Gather the children around you and the easel. Introduce the book to the children by pointing out the title of the book, the author, the illustrator, and the title page. Tell them that as you read, they will need to be detectives to watch for certain things.

Read them a giant book and track the words with your finger as you read. When you have finished, go back to page one and introduce the idea of a sentence. Show the children that a sentence is something you say that tells someone something. It begins with a capital letter. When you have read the sentence, a dot called a "period" shows the end of what you have said. Your voice drops when you reach a period. Read a sentence and have the children echo your expression as you come to the end of the sentence.

Practice with the children finding each sentence and marking its beginning and its ending. Read aloud and the children will echo each sentence you find.

LESSON - Writing sentences

Have the children get comfortable on a firm writing surface, and begin to dictate the list of words and phrases provided for you below. Give them plenty of time to write, and as they do, check for those who need to gain more focus on their work. Be sure and have the children sound as they write! When dictating to young children it is helpful at first to select words in families so the children will move easily from one to the other. For example, start with lists of words that end the same. When you are going to move to another family, tell them you are doing so.

Words to dictate: a, at, am, on, the, I, cat, sat, fat, mat, Sam, am, Pam, cap, map, mop, pop, mom, cop, stop.

Phrases and sentences to dictate:

A cat.
A mat.
A fat cat.
The cat sat.
The cat sat on a mat.
The fat cat sat on Sam.
The cat sat on the mop.

I sat on the cap.
Sam sat on the map.
Pat sat on the mat.
I sat on Mom.

An alternative to writing every sentence is to provide the child with a sentence written on a strip then cut into words. The child will lay the words out in front of him and as you say each word in the sentence, he will locate the word and place it in front of him. By the time he's located all the words in the sentence as you say them, he will have created the sentence correctly.

JOURNALING

On a clean page in their journal, have the children draw a picture of anything they want and then write the words that go with their picture. They may refer to the words in the pocket chart if they run out of ideas.

WORD GAMES

• Sentence Unscramble - have short sentences on little cards in baggies for the children to lay out and put in the correct order. (R35)

• Matching Picture to Sentence - Provide copies of picture match sheets for children to work on. They will cut out the pictures and paste them under the sentence that tells what is in the picture. (R32)

• Making Sentences - a small group of children can work together at the pocket chart constructing sentences out of the word cards there.

• Use the Bingo game from R31.

• Use books, newspaper, magazines and have children do a Word Search, recording on a paper the words they find that they know.

• Matching Words - a group of children can do a Making Words activity where they cut apart the words at the bottom of the sheet and paste them under the pictures that illustrate each word. (Ex: CAP under the picture of the cap) (R33)

• Sound Hunt - Put the sounds the children know on a piece of paper and have them hunt with a partner for items that begin with the sounds of their letters. Challenge them to find 3 for each letter!

• Go Fish - Use the Go Fish cards provided for this first game and play the game. Children will not only have to read the word on their card in order to ask for what they want, but the others will need to be able to sort through their cards to find the word. (R34)

LET'S MOVE!

With the whole class on their feet, call out words and have the children bodyspell them accompanied by the letter sounds. After a bit of practice, try partnering up the children so that they can take turns calling out a word for their partner. Something that will help in this endeavor is to give the "caller" a few cards to use in calling words. That way both children are reviewing!

19

OBJECTIVES
1. Child will review 8 letter sounds
2. Child will practice blending the sounds
3. Child will alter words to make new words
4. Child will review sight words

MATERIALS

1. Plain sight word cards learned to date
2. Letter blocks or cards for each student
3. Bingo Games (R37, p. 84)
4. Lily pad games (R38, pp. 85, 87, 89)
5. Word Search sheets (R36, p. 83)
6. Tapes for two *centers on which sounds and words are dictated for independent use. (see center descriptions)
7. Room arranged in four *centers, children divided into four groups
8. Timer

ANTicipatory SET

Introduce this lesson by talking about how athletes show what they can do by playing games with other individuals or teams. These games can be anything from T-ball in the afternoon to Olympic games. Explain that today you are going to have your own special classroom Olympic games with four different events! Show the children how each center will work. Arrange them into four groups using a color or animal to identify them. Show them your timer and let them hear the bell so that they will know what to listen for as they finish one center and prepare to move to the next. Tell them how to switch to the new center. (In the beginning I had the children stand by their chairs upon hearing the bell, then move as a group to the next center. Doing this will prevent the class from running amok in their excitement and leaving you to sort them out again!)

LET THE GAMES BEGIN!

Lily Pad Center:
Each child has a game board and frogs to use. One child is assigned to push "play." On the tape, you will have recorded sounds that the children have learned (NOT letter names) with a significant pause between each sound. When the children hear a sound, they will look on their board for the lilypad that has the picture of that sound. They will put a frog on that lilypad.

You may choose to tape three versions of the sounds so the children can play three times. When they have played the third time, your voice on the tape will direct them to press "stop" and then "rewind." Of course, you will need to teach these skills to the children ahead of time. (R38, three pages)

Bingo Center:
If you have a parent or aide to help you, let the adult call out the words the children will be looking for. If there is

no adult, use a pre-recorded tape again, allowing enough time between words for the children to hunt and mark the words. It would be great to have the tape AND an adult helper (or volunteer from an upper el classroom) so the children can get used to doing this activity independently. (R37)

Word Search Center:
This center will be done independently by the children. Each child will take a sheet containing the words, a marker or crayon, and will identify the words hidden inside the grid. They may use a partner for this activity, or consult with each other for whisper help. (R36)

Word Morph Center:
This center is led by the teacher. Each child in front of you will have a set of letters from which to choose. You may want to give them two sets just in case. Follow these or similar steps:

1. Spell AT
2. Add one letter so it spells SAT
3. Change one letter so it spells SAP
4. Change one letter so it spells TAP
5. Change one letter to spell TOP
6. Change one letter to spell TOT
7. Change one letter to spell POT
8. Change one letter to spell PAT
9. Change one letter to spell FAT
10. Change one letter to spell SAT
11. Change one letter to spell SAM
12. Change one letter to spell PAM

Continue on in this fashion. To add extra challenge to this game, include four-letter words (always sounding out) such as STOP, SPOT, SPAT, SCOT, SPAM, SCAT, FAST, PAST, MAST, CAST.

MORE
For students who are advanced: Provide them with letter cards and sight words. Have them:
1. Form as many words as they can with the letters, writing the words down on blank cards
2. Create sentences using their word cards
3. Place their sentences in the pocket chart to share
4. Illustrate the sentences they write
5. Create their own version of stylized words to share
6. Create a poster together using their words and illustration that goes with their writing.

*For homeschool setting, ignore references to centers and just enjoy the activities with your child.

20 📖 Book 1 - A Cat

OBJECTIVES
1. Child will successfully read *A Cat*
2. Child will write the story line from dictation
3. Child will make sentences using words from the book

MATERIALS

1. *A Cat,* six copies
2. Sentence strips for the book text
3. Word cards from the story
4. Blank books for each child
5. "Stocked" centers
6. Resource 39 (p. 91)

ANTICIPATORY SET

Build excitement in the children by reminding them of all the words they can read already! Ask them if they think they can read a book now. Wait for comments! Say, "We are going to find out today if you can read a book already! I think you can!"

LESSON

Draw attention to the pocket chart in which you have placed the sentences in rows; one row per page in the book. Have the children do a bit of noticing before you read. See if they can find words that appear more than one time (cat is a good one to hunt for!). Ask them how they can recognize the word cat quickly. (Draw attention to the ending of the word, and remind the children that any time they come to a word that ends in AT, they don't really have to sound out the word, except to notice the sound the word starts with.) Point out the AT words and practice with the children noticing the AT out loud, then adding the initial sound. Let a few children try this activity on their own.

Now, invite the children to read the lines with you. When you are finished, be sure and clap for each other! You are going to break into groups and meet with the children one group at a time to read from the real books.

WRITING

Using their whiteboards, dictate parts of the book for the children to write. After each sentence is written, ask them to hold up their boards for you to see. Let children take turns reading their sentence to the class after each sentence you dictate.

FOLLOW-UP

Prepare the children for breaking into groups and working in centers. I would recommend starting with your group that needs the most support from you so that they will have more guidance and teacher-directed practice before they are expected to rotate to another center. I would schedule my most advanced group last, starting them on a center such as Pocket Chart Center

or Go Fish Center. I would recommend assigning a leader to each group, and would instruct them on how to help monitor their own group. This responsibility can change as children demonstrate their ability to be a great example to their peers.

CENTERS

Teacher Center:

Give each child at the table a copy of the book *A Cat*. Instruct the children to follow along closely, tracking with their pointer finger as you all read together. First read the title of the book, the author, then open to the title page. Repeat the process there. Turn to the first page and make sure everyone's pointer finger is on the first word. Read together. Repeat this process through all the pages.

After reading the book together, decide whether you want each child to take a turn reading the book, or if you want partners to read aloud together, taking turns.

It is critical to instill in your students the habit of making mental pictures of what they read. To this end, instruct the children to read one sentence and then close their eyes and make a picture in their mind of what they read. Visualization is the foundation for reading comprehension when passages become more advanced and children have to read for content. Time spent early building the skill of visualization will pay rich dividends over time.

Pocket Chart Center:

Leave cards with words from the book in the pocket chart and let the group there make their own sentences using the word cards. They should record the sentence they build in their center folders. (I viewed center folders as the children's accountability piece to me. I did rapid daily checks to be sure the children were on task during centers. You want to establish "on task" from day one so teaching and learning will happen in your room!)

Word Search Center:

Use the sheet provided for this lesson and copy enough for each child to have one. The completed sheet should be stored in a center folder for you to check. (R39)

Go Fish Center:

If you have taught the children to play Go Fish, provide this center with cards with which to play. Alternatively, they could draw and write in their journals, or do independent "reading" of books. You could also elect to have them word hunt for a specific word or words in newspapers, or any other such word activity, including teaching programs on the computer, if you have that resource available to you.

Wrap-Up:

Give the children their blank books and have them work under your guidance to make their own *A Cat* books. They need to write the title, their name as author and illustrator, and then they will write the storyline and illustrate each page. They can work on this project for a few days, then take it home to read to parents.

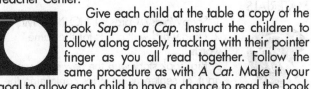

OBJECTIVES
1. Child will successfully read *Sap on a Cap*
2. Child will write the story line from dictation
3. Child will make sentences using words from the book

MATERIALS

1. *Sap on a Cap*, six copies
2. Sentence strips for the book text
3. Word cards from the story
4. Drawing paper for each child
5. "Stocked" centers
6. Resource 40 (p. 92), R34 (p.81)

ANTICIPATORY SET

If you can find a piece of bark with sap on it, please bring it in to share with the children. Some of them will have experienced the sticky-yuckiness of sap as they were playing around a tree, but many will not have encountered this substance before. Talk about the fact that in the woods there might be trees with sap on the trunks. Share that you are going to read another book today, and this time it is about a little boy who is camping in the woods and finds sap on the trees!

LESSON

Draw attention to the pocket chart in which you have placed the sentences from the book in rows; one row per page in the book. Before you start, do a scan of the words like you did in the last lesson, where children notice the endings of words. You can find words with matching endings, find words that appear more than once, and model for the children how we can scan a book before we read it to find out as much as we can about what is inside.

Now, invite the children to read the lines with you. Let volunteers take turns reading the strips as time permits.

WRITING

Using their whiteboards, dictate parts of the book for the children to write. After each sentence is written, ask them to hold up their boards for you to see. Let children take turns reading their sentence to the class after each sentence you dictate.

FOLLOW-UP

Today you will follow the same procedure as the last lesson in which you have groups, an order in which they will rotate, a leader for each group, and so forth. Praise your children for even traces of good performance during centers on the previous day, and briefly share with them the areas in which they can do even better! I learned from my first principal to "praise approximate

performance"--as though it was perfection itself, as this recognition gives the child the fuel and internal motivation to keep on striving for better and better execution of desired behaviors!

CENTERS:
Teacher Center:

Give each child at the table a copy of the book *Sap on a Cap*. Instruct the children to follow along closely, tracking with their pointer finger as you all read together. Follow the same procedure as with *A Cat*. Make it your goal to allow each child to have a chance to read the book on his own with the other children tracking silently with him as he reads.

If time does not allow for individual reading, let the children read to their partner right there at your center, or have three readings, with partners alternating pages.

Again, be sure and take time to practice visualization. (See Teacher Center Lesson 20).

Pocket Chart Center:

Leave cards with words from the book in the pocket chart and let the group there make their own sentences using the word cards. They should record the sentence they build in their center folders.

Word Search Center:

Use the sheet provided for this lesson and copy enough for each child to have one. (R40)

Go Fish Center:

Use R34.

Wrap-Up:

Give the children a blank sheet of paper and let them draw a picture of themselves camping in the woods like Sam did in our story. They should label their drawing as usual. Allow for share time.

Those that finish early may grab a partner and read the book again together.

ACROSS THE CURRICULUM

• Science - Study structure of a tree -- and learn about the way sap rises. Sap starts running when the days are warm but the nights are still cold. So whenever you see sap buckets on maple trees, spring isn't far away.

Related study - the enormous value of trees in sustaining life on this planet, rainforests, etc.

22 in, no, not, me, by

OBJECTIVES
1. Child will review sight words learned to date
2. Child will learn sight words in, no, not, me, by
3. Child will find sight words in print
4. Child will use sight words in sentences

MATERIALS

1. SnapWords® Cards IN, NO, NOT, ME, BY
2. Plain word wall cards for the same words
3. Big book story with the new sight words in it, or sentences on strips containing the sight words for today
4. Newsprint or old magazines, scissors, yellow crayons
5. Resource 41 (p. 93)

ANTicipatory SET

With the children around you, place the new SnapWords® in the pocket chart in plain view of all the children. Tell them you are going to play a game with the new words.

LESSON - Sight Words IN, NO, NOT, ME, BY

Let the children talk about the visuals on the words. Notice the similarities between NO and NOT. Play around with the words, using the motion and the sentences on the reverse of the cards.

Then, play a game with the students called, "No, not me!" Choose a place in the room to be the pantry. This should be a place not easily seen by the group when they are sitting on the rug. Choose one child to go there before the game starts. Then tell the children to pretend that you just baked some brownies and have placed them on a plate to cool in the pantry. Pretend to be washing dishes, and then "hear" a noise coming from the pantry. "Are YOU in the pantry, Jane?" you call (use a name from your class, but not the child that is actually in the pantry. The child [Jane] should answer, "No, not me! I'm BY the pantry!" Continue calling names of children in the class until finally you call the name of the child who is hiding in the pantry. When you call his name, he will answer, "Yes it's me! I'm *in* the pantry!"

After the students have viewed the stylized side of the cards for a while, show them the plain sides of the cards. Have them practice reading the words on the plain side. If they make a mistake, just quickly flip the card over to the stylized side to give them a brief peek.

VISUAL IMPRINTING

Have the children identify the words from the plain side, but then ask them - if they are correct - how they remembered the word. Ask them what the visual was. Have them close their eyes, see the SnapWord™ in their minds, and then describe what they see.

WRITING

Have the children write their new sight words in their journals as you dictate them. Show them the stylized word for a couple of seconds. Have them close their eyes and "see" the word in their minds, then quickly open their eyes and write what they saw on their whiteboards.

FOLLOW-UP

Children can make their own version of stylized SnapWords® Cards. They could also use their journals to draw pictures of their favorite animals in, on, or by something. They should label each picture with the correct location word. They could make a really nice sequence of picture/sentences using their new sight words. They won't know they are writing prepositional phrases, but they will be!

EX: "A cat on the [picture of object]."
"A cat in the [picture of object]."
"A cat by the [picture of object]."

They could do the same activity using their own name instead of the words "A cat."

CENTERS
Teacher Center

Use this time to do assessments for decoding, segmenting, sound recognition, both oral and written.

Other centers should be created based on where you feel extra help is needed for each of your groups.

See Resource 41 for a making-words activity. These words may form a center as often as you feel the children need the practice in forming words.

EXTRA HELPS

• Distinguishing between ME and MY - These two words have caused a lot of trouble for little people for many years. Why not give them a visual and motion to help out? The jingle for ME and MY goes like this: "ME has an E, MY has a Y." Refer to page 103 in the Resources for Section One for a visual, auditory and kinesthetic reminder for distinguishing between ME and MY.

ASSESSMENT

Assess for sight word recognition, adding our new words to the S.T. form when you feel the children are able to recognize the word on sight.

23 Book 3 - Tot in a Cot

OBJECTIVES
1. Child will successfully read *Tot in a Cot*
2. Child will write the story line from dictation
3. Child will make sentences using words from the book

MATERIALS

1. *Tot in a Cot*, six copies
2. Sentence strips for the book text
3. Word cards from the story
4. Drawing paper for each child
5. "Stocked" centers
6. Dry, clean rag mop and clean bucket
7. Resources 42-43 (pp. 94-95)

ANTICIPATORY SET

Set the stage for reading this book by finding out how many of your children have a younger sibling at home. Explain to them that sometimes we call toddlers "tots." Ask them if they have ever heard anyone say "tot" before. Show them how the word looks by writing it on your whiteboard, and ask how many "tools" are needed to build this word. (only two distinct tools... an O and 2 T's). Bodyspell the word TOT together and brainstorm other words they can think of that might rhyme with TOT (cot, got, hot, lot, jot, not, pot, rot). Emphasize that the reason these words rhyme is because of the two letter ending OT. Have the children close their eyes and "see" TOT in their minds.

LESSON

Draw attention to the pocket chart in which you have placed the sentences from the book in rows; one row per page in the book. Before you start, do a scan of the words again, looking for all the OT words. Remind the children that they already know how to read OT, so if they see a word that ends in OT, they just have to sound what comes in front of it, and blend it into the OT ending.

Now, invite the children to read the lines with you. Let volunteers take turns to read the strips as time permits.

WRITING

Using their whiteboards, dictate parts of the book for the children to write. After each sentence written, ask them to hold up their boards for you to see. Let children take turns reading their sentence to the class after each sentence you dictate.

FOLLOW-UP

Today you will follow the same procedure as the last lesson in which you have groups, an order in which they will rotate, a leader for each group, and so forth. Use this time to praise them for even approximately good performance on centers last time, and again, share with them the areas in which they can do even better,

realizing children are learning a new skill!

CENTERS
Teacher Center:

Give each child at the table a copy of the book *Tot in a Cot*. Instruct the children to follow along closely, tracking with their pointer finger as you all read together. Follow the same procedure as with previous books. Make it your goal to allow each child to have a chance to read the book on his own with the other children tracking silently with him as he reads.

If time does not allow for individual reading, let pairs of children read to each other until all have read.

Remember to practice visualization.

Pocket Chart Center:

Leave cards with words from the book in the pocket chart and let the group there make their own sentences using the word cards. They should record the sentence they build in their center folders for you to check. Add cards with the plain sight words they have learned to date to give them more options for sentence-building.

What is it? Center:

Use the sheet provided for this lesson and copy enough for each child to have one. There will be pictures of items and under each picture there are lines on which the children will write the letters that form the word shown in the picture. When they are finished, they can color the pictures. (R42)

Word Sort Center:

Word sorting is a great way to reinforce fluency in reading. I always kept an extensive card file of words written on 3x5" cards so I could just pull out a group of cards with target spellings for the children to sort. For today, for example, the 4th center could have two sets of words, half the cards with OT endings and half with endings from another word family such as OP or AT. The children will have the task of sorting the cards into families and then recording how they sorted the words. If you would like to add a third word family, the children doubtless could sort the cards into families.

I did not tell the students what the word families were, I just let them figure that out together. They always could! When I worked in small groups, I found the children loved it when I put them into a circle and tossed the cards in the air and let them "rain" down to the floor. They rushed over, turned all the words face up, then as quickly as possible, sorted the cards into families. This was so much fun for them! (R43 -- and you might want to enlarge the page when you copy it)

Wrap-up:
Act out the story with the mop and bucket!

24 📖 Book 4 - Fat Cat

OBJECTIVES
1. Child will successfully read *Fat Cat*
2. Child will write the story line from dictation
3. Child will make sentences using words from the book

MATERIALS

1. *Fat Cat*, six copies
2. Sentence strips for the book text
3. Word cards from the story
4. Drawing paper for each child
5. "Stocked" centers
6. Big pot or box with lid

ANTICIPATORY SET

Set the stage for reading this book by discussing the phrase, "Curiosity killed the cat." Ask them what curiosity means. Discuss their answers. Then discuss the link between "curiosity killed the cat" and the other phrase "A cat has nine lives!" Do they think that if cats are curious they might get themselves into trouble at times? Tell them that they will be reading a book today about a cat that was very curious and got into a bit of trouble as a result!

LESSON

Draw attention to the pocket chart in which you have placed the sentences from the book in rows. Discuss together the word families they notice in the sentences. Now, read the strips together. Let volunteers take turns to read the strips as time permits. If the children are interested in telling about times in which they might have gotten into a jam because of their curiosity, allow for share time as time permits!

Use the box or pot you brought with you and a small object to review the "position words" of ON, BY, and IN. Expand the lesson by introducing other position words and demonstrating what they mean (behind, in front, under, over, etc.)

WRITING

Using their whiteboards, dictate parts of the book for the children to write. After each sentence written, ask them to hold up their boards for you to see. Let children take turns reading their sentence to the class after each sentence you dictate.

FOLLOW-UP

Today you will follow the same procedure as before, always refining on the smooth flow of the centers. Consider rewarding groups that work well with free time to do a game together such as Go Fish or War.

CENTERS
Teacher Center:

Give each child at the table a copy of the book *Fat Cat*. After the initial reading of the book together, let each child have a turn to read alone, even if it is just a page or two. Focus on moving from decoding each word to just recognizing the word.

You can reinforce this skill by taking individual words from the book, holding up a card and asking the child to guess the word instantly rather than decoding. If you hold up a card on which is written POT, and the child says CAT, ask, "Can this really say CAT? Do you see the sound of Ccc at the beginning?" Lead them into the skill of quickly scanning initial sound and word family as they are reading. Their decoding would sound like this: C-AT rather than C-A-T.

If they need even more practice, take your word family cards (cat, sat, pat, fat, mat) and flash them quickly one after the other as the children read them. Keep to word families and tell the children the word family you are doing before you start. Tell them ALL they have to look at is the beginning sound and add it to the word family ending. The point of this exercise is to move children towards understanding that they can recognize words instantly and do not always have to decode! Some children come to believe that because we teach them to decode, they have to decode everything, even if they don't need to!

Yet another way to reinforce fluency is by the use of whiteboards... small group or whole group. SAY, "we are going to write some AT family words. First word is..." call out the list of AT family words you have and let the children write them in a column on their whiteboards. When you switch word families, tell them you are switching. If you write a word family column on your whiteboard, use one color for the onset and a different color for the rime.

Pocket Chart Center:
Same procedure as before.

Making Words Center:
Same procedure as before.

Word Sort Center:
Same procedure as before.

Wrap-up or alternate 4th center:
Children can draw an object or pet in the various positions you discussed in your lesson (on, by, in, over, under, etc).

25 and, go, is*

© 2007 Sarah Major

OBJECTIVES
1. Child will review all sight words learned to date
2. Child will learn sight words AND, GO, IS
3. Child will find sight words in print
4. Child will use sight words in sentences

MATERIALS

1. SnapWords® Cards for AND, GO, IS
2. SnapWords® Cards for all words to date
3. Plain word wall cards for all of Group 1 words (from Appendix B)
4. The book, *Marvin K Mooney, Will You Please Go Now!*
5. Activities to Teach Sight Words, Appendix A

ANTicipatory SET

With the children around you, place all the List A Group 1 words in the pocket chart in front of you (a, and, at, by, go, in, is, me, no, not, on, the). You should display the stylized side first. Tell the children you are going to play some games.

Start by reading the story book, *Marvin K Mooney*, and point out the various instances of the word GO!

LESSON - Sight Words AND, GO, IS

Let the children talk about the visuals on the words. Doubtless by this time, they will have no trouble identifying the word GO.

Point out that although IS has a picture of Sss at the end, it really SOUNDS like a fizzy snake, not a hissing snake! Practice saying the word IS together, feeling the buzz on your tongues! Display the words IN and IS together and notice the fact that they start with the same sound, and can be used in sentences together. (The cat IS IN the box.")

Put NO and GO together and discover that they rhyme! (chant, "NO I will not GO!")

Practice making oral sentences using the sight words.

It is now time to transition to all plain words. Play **Word Flip** (activity 9). Children will vote on which card to turn over forever! Do this one at a time until all 12 words are on the plain sides of the cards. Next, play **Pop Up** (activity 2).

WRITING

Finally, give the children sheets of paper and pencils, have them use their whiteboards as desks, and give a formal assessment.

They should number their papers in a column, numbers 1-12, or give them paper already numbered. Call out one sight word at a time, saying, "Find and write GO." "Find and write ME." Continue until all the words have been found and written. Collect and grade, recording the scores. Identify words for more practice.

FOLLOW-UP

Ask the children to write their new sight words in their journals. Also ask them to select 3-4 words to use in making a sentence they will write and then illustrate in their journals. Get them started with these ideas, if they are having trouble coming up with ideas on their own:
"The cat is in...[picture]."
"The cat is by me." (wow! 5 words!)
"Fat cat is not by me."
"Fat cat is on [picture of object]."
"A cat is in [picture of object]."
"No cat is in [picture of something with no cat!]"

GRADUATION!

Tell the children that you are now finished with group 1 words and it is time they graduated to the classroom word wall! Make a big ceremony out of posting the plain, green words to the word wall while they are watching. Next, take out List A Group 2 SnapWords® cards and make a ceremony out of putting them into the pocket chart! Doubtless the children will be excited to see the new words, so spend a few minutes discovering them together. Read the word, do the motion and read the sentence on the back. More tomorrow!

EXTRA HELPS - looking ahead to lesson 26

• **Distinguishing between IT and IS/ NO and ON** - These two pairs of words have caused a lot of trouble with my students over the years when they are confronted with the words IT and IS in different sequence, such as in a statement (it is) vs. a question (is it). I am not clear on why the confusion, exactly, only that it happens! The children will have the sight word IT in the next lesson. Same goes for ON and NO. I can see the issue there because we have the same letters, but reversed.

It might help to play a game. Write the four words on cards, and before you play, analyze the words together. Point out that IT and IS start the same, but that they can tell in an instant which is which because of the endings! So they will need to be detectives and glance at the end before saying the word. Point out that ON and NO have the same exact letters, and they will be detectives by checking out the start sound before they say the word. As you talk about ON and NO, cover the ending when speaking of the initial sound, and cover the initial sound when talking about the ending. You might want to write the initial sound in green and the end sound in red.

After the introduction of these words, flash one card at a time for them to read quickly. Every couple of times, stop and shuffle the cards to change their order.

Another idea that might make a difference is to have the children read IS and make the body motion for S, and then read IT and make the body motion for T as they read.

26 to, it, up, sit

OBJECTIVES
1. Child will review word wall words
2. Child will learn sight words TO, IT, UP, SIT
3. Child will find sight words in print
4. Child will use sight words in sentences

MATERIALS

1. SnapWords® Cards for TO, IT, UP, SIT
2. SnapWords® Cards, List A Group 2
3. Plain word wall cards for target sight words for today.
4. The book: *Great Day for Up*
5. Newsprint or old magazines, scissors, yellow crayons.
6. Resource 44 (p. 96)

ANTicipatory SET

Gather the children around you and the List A Group 2 SnapWords® in the pocket chart. (it, sit, to, up, or, help, I, my, see, now, do, he). Tell the children you are going to play some games with them, but first they will have a story!

Read *Great Day for Up*. When you have finished, or as you are at a good place to pause, let the children find all the UPs on a page. It is doubtful they will have trouble learning that word after hearing and seeing this story!

LESSON - Sight Words TO, IT, UP, SIT

Warm up by playing **Pop Up** (p. 282) for a few minutes. Alternative games are activities **Around the World** and **Which is Which?**

When you are ready to focus on today's words, ask the children to find the two words that rhyme (it and sit). Ask them why they rhyme.

Show them TO and point out that TO does not rhyme with NO and GO from last lesson. Tell them that they will have a word DO very soon that does rhyme with TO so they don't have to worry about TO not having a friend!

WRITING

Have the children look and write their way through the sight words for today. They will study the stylized side of the sight word and then look down to write, not referring back to the stylized word. If a child says, "I can't remember," ask him/her to close their eyes first and see if they can remember the picture in their minds. Don't make them wait more than a couple of seconds before letting them refer back to the stylized sight word. The reason for this is that for a child to copy a word by looking at it yields very little in the way of real learning. If they can rely on another modality for recalling what they have seen, they will truly have gained a lot in the process of learning how they learn!

FOLLOW-UP

Ask the children to select 3-4 words to use in making a sentence they will write and then illustrate. Get them started with these ideas, if they are having trouble coming up with ideas on their own:

"Go and sit by a...[picture of object]."
"It is up on the [picture of object]."
"The fat cat is not up on [picture of object]."
"It is up on a... [picture of object]."

Have the children also write their new sight words in their journals.

CENTERS

Pocket Chart Center:
Same procedure as before, including new sight words.

Making Words Center:
Supply the center with letter cards or plastic letters and challenge the children to make as many words as possible.

Word Sort Center:
This center will need cards with decodable, word family words for the children to sort.

Scavenger Hunt:
This group will have the newspapers or magazines and will be hunting for their new sight words.

Sentence Unscramble:
Children will have short sentences written on little cards, cut up, and stored in baggies for them to take turns assembling in their center. When they have figured out one sentence, they should write it in their center folder or journal, and then switch baggies with another child. Make sure they know to watch for capital letters to start their sentence, and end marks to end their sentence. The other words fill in the middle like the jelly on a sandwich! See R44.

The teacher could use this time to supervise the centers and assess individual students.

OBJECTIVES
1. Child will successfully read *Pat and Matt*
2. Child will write the story line from dictation
3. Child will make sentences using words from the book

MATERIALS

1. *Pat and Matt*, six copies
2. Sentence strips for the book text
3. Word cards from the story
4. Drawing paper for each child
5. "Stocked" centers
6. Copy of *Blueberries for Sal*
7. Resource 45

ANTICIPATORY SET

Set the stage for reading this book by reading *Blueberries For Sal*, in which a bear cub and a human cub meet each other at the top of a hill while picking blueberries. Tell the children something a bit like this is going to happen in our story for today.

LESSON

Draw attention to the pocket chart in which you have placed the sentences from the book in rows. Do an analysis of the words from this book to see what they notice. You will need to point out the difference between mat and Matt. The name is identified by a capital letter, but it also has a double T at the end. A mat with no capital letter and only one T is something like a rug.

The children might struggle with the sequence of words in this book: IS IT or IT IS. If they do, consider playing the game described in the right column of lesson 25. Let the children practice orally making sentences and questions using the two sequences of words. Point out that when you ask a question, you are trying to find something out and your voice might go up on the end. If you say IT IS, you already know, and you are telling someone else.

WRITING

Dictate parts of the book for the children to write on their whiteboards. After each sentence written, say, "Boards up!" so you can do a quick visual check. Let children take turns reading their sentence to the class after each sentence you dictate.

FOLLOW-UP

Today you will follow the same procedure as before, always refining on the smooth flow of the centers. Consider rewarding groups that work well with free time to do a game together such as Go Fish or War. It would be great to take a minute between switching centers to do a very rapid visual scan of what the centers are doing - maybe you can check one group between each center you lead... for the sake of accountability.

CENTERS
Teacher Center:

Give each child at the table a copy of the book *Pat and Matt*. Again, focus on moving from decoding each word to just saying the word. Teach the children to use two tools to help them: 1] check for what would make sense, and 2] do a quick look at the word to pick a clue, such as an initial sound or a final word family.

It might be valuable to repeat the following from Lesson 24 as often as you feel the children need it: *(it is reprinted here as a quick reminder if needed).*

Again, you can reinforce this skill by taking individual words from the book, holding up a card and asking the child to guess the word instantly rather than decoding. If you hold up a card on which is written POT, and the child says CAT, ask, "Can this really say CAT? Do you see the sound of Ccc at the beginning?" Lead them into the skill of quickly scanning initial sound and word family as they are reading. Their decoding would sound like this: C-AT rather than C-A-T.

If they need even more practice, take your word family cards (cat, sat, pat, fat, mat) and flash them quickly one after the other as the children read them. Keep to word families and tell the children the word family you are doing before you start. Tell them ALL they have to look at is the beginning sound and add it to the word family ending.

Be sure and make it very clear when you are switching word families (such as from AT words to OT words).

Yet another way to reinforce fluency is by the use of whiteboards... small group or whole group. SAY, "we are going to write some AT family words. First word is..." Call out the list of AT family words you have and let the children write them in a column on their whiteboards. When you switch word families, tell them you are switching. If you write a word family column on your whiteboard, use one color for the onset and a different color for the rhyme.

Pocket Chart Center:

A great variation for the pocket chart center is for you to quickly make make sentences for each row of the pocket chart. Leave the sentence mixed up, words in a stack. The children will need to cooperate in making the sentence for each row of the pocket chart. They will record the results in their center folder.

Sentence Unscramble Center: (R45)

Story Wrap-up:

Children can draw their own idea of what they would like to meet by accident on top of a hill, or they can draw what they think the kids who met could have done instead of a picnic.

OBJECTIVES
1. Child will successfully read *Mat on a Tot*
2. Child will write the story line from dictation
3. Child will practice identifying questions, statements, and exclamations
4. Child will learn to write question marks and exclamation points.

MATERIALS

1. *Mat on a Tot*, six copies
2. Sentence strips for the book text
3. Stylized SnapWords® Card for OR
4. Clean rug or mat for acting out story
5. "Stocked" centers
6. Big book with punctuation marks: ! ? .
7. Resources 46-48 if needed (pp. 98-100)

ANTICIPATORY SET

Read your big book selection, making sure to read with expression. Just enjoy the story. When you have finished, go back through the book and point out the punctuation marks. Say, "Did you know that there are special marks in books that are like clues? Let me show you some." Find a question mark and tell the children its name. Tell the children that the ? is used when someone wants to know something. When we read a question, we raise our voice at the end because we are showing that we really don't know!

Re-read the sentence, then ask the children to echo you, copying your inflection.

Find a period and share with the children that when this mark is used, it just marks the end of something that we were told. Practice reading and echoing as before.

Find an exclamation point and teach concept. This is a mark that shows feeling! Read and echo as before.

LESSON - Sight word OR

Write the following on your whiteboard: "? or ! or ." Show the children SnapWord™ OR and talk about how we use the word. In the picture a boy is trying to decide which toy he wants. Tell the children you are going to play a detective game and they will be choosing [read the phrase on the whiteboard again, emphasizing the word OR]. Tell them you are going to read some sentences and they will need to tell you if it is a question, OR a statement, OR an exclamation. They will be identifying one type of sentence at a time. First listen for exclamation points. If they hear a sentence with an exclamation at the end, they should give you the silent thumbs up. Repeat the sentences for ? Finally, ask them to identify statements.

"I am Mrs. Swift."
"Are you hungry?"
"It is so hot in here!"
"Is it time to eat yet?"
"I'm so scared!"
"I need to cook dinner."
"What are we going to do today?"
"I can't wait to go to the zoo!"
"My dog's name is Marshall."

Read the *Mat on a Tot* sentence strips together as in other lessons, paying close attention to inflection as you read. You might want to do the reading and have them echo you the first time through.

WRITING

Dictate parts of the book for the children to write on their whiteboards. After each sentence, say, "Boards up!" so you can do a quick visual check. Let children take turns reading their sentence to the class after each sentence you dictate.

Have the children practice the formation of the punctuation marks on their whiteboards. Question marks always present a challenge, so encourage the children to stick out their left pointer finger to draw around in order to get the top of the question mark nice and round. Have them write OR in their journals.

CENTERS
Teacher Center:
Give each child at the table a copy of the book *Mat on a Tot*. Scan the book before reading it, noting the types of words, counting how many ? they find, etc.

Again, focus on moving from decoding each word to just saying the word. Review the use of two tools to help them: 1] check for what would make sense, and 2] do a quick look at the word to pick a clue, such as an initial sound or a final word family.

Repeat the drill from Lesson 24 as often as you feel the children need it.

Make-a-Book Center:
Children will make a little book with a drawing on each page: The mat on top of something we cannot see. The words on the page should involve the practicing of ? and ! and . (Ex: "Is it a cat?" "No! It is not a cat!")

Scavenger Hunt:
Each group that rotates through this center will have the opportunity to cut ? and ! from old magazines or newspapers and glue them onto a large sheet of paper. By the time the four groups have rotated through, you should have one poster that the whole class collaborated in making. Display on a bulletin board while you are continuing to practice these punctuation marks.

Journal:
Have the children draw two pictures that would show two things they are choosing between. They should write a big OR between the two pictures.

Whole group activity:
Use the rug you brought to have the children take turns acting out the story, a group at a time. Have one child hide under the mat, and then have the class ask the question, "Is it Peter?" and Peter would answer, "No, not me!" etc. Finally ask if it is the child who is actually under the mat. All of you then finish the play by exclaiming, "It IS Fred!"

29 do, my, see, help, he, I

OBJECTIVES
1. Child will review word wall words & new words
2. Child will learn sight words DO, MY, SEE, HELP, HE, I
3. Child will find sight words in print
4. Child will use sight words in sentences

MATERIALS

1. SnapWords® Cards for new words
2. Plain word wall cards for target sight words for today.
5. Poster for ME and MY (R51 p. 103)
6. Newsprint or old magazines, scissors, yellow crayons.
7. Resources 49-53 (pp. 101-106)

ANTICIPATORY SET

Gather the children around you and the List A Group 2 SnapWords® in the pocket chart. (it, sit, to, up, or, help, I, my, see, now, do, he). Arrange four of the words like this: "I DO SEE MY..." and let the children read the phrase with you and then fill in the blank with what they see that is theirs. A fun game would be to toss a little bean bag to a child who will make a sentence that starts with those words. He then will toss the bean bag to another child who will take his turn making a sentence.

LESSON - Sight Words DO, MY, SEE, HELP, HE, I.

Warm up by playing Pop Up (p. 282) for a few minutes. Alternative games are Activities, Around the World and Which is Which? *

When you are ready to focus on today's words, ask the children to find the two words that rhyme (HE and SEE). Put the word ME with them. Say, "HE can SEE ME!"

Point out that SEE has two Es and chant, "See has 2 Es" while pointing to the two e's on the SnapWords® Card.

Display TO and DO together and exlaim dramatically, "What am I TO DO?"

Display GO and NO together and say, "She said NO, I can't GO!"

Display ME and MY together and explore the poster together that will help them distinguish between the two words. Have them practice saying the little jingle while doing the motions for ME and MY.

Display HELP and practice the motion and language. Let the children tell you why they think the "person" in the water is yelling HELP!

WRITING

Have the children look and write their way through the sight words for today. They will study the stylized side of the sight word and then look down to write, without referring back to the stylized word. Display the sight words in rhyming groups (he, me, see; I, my; to, do). Point out that

they can rely on their imaginations to write the word help. Have them write their new sight words in their journals. Remember to encourage children to "see" the word in their minds before writing it.

CENTERS
Teacher Center:
Use this time for working with children who need extra help in decoding, sight word recognition, letter formation, or use the time to begin individual assessments of sight words or solo reading while the class rotates through the four centers.

Pocket Chart Center:
Making sentences with sight words to write in center folders.

Scavenger Hunt:
Children will look for their new sight words in print, cut them out and glue on paper, or highlight them with a yellow crayon.

Book Center:
Children in this center will take turns reading books 1-6 to each other.

Bingo:
Same procedure as before. (R49)

See other Resources to use for centers as needed: R50, R52, and R53.

*See also Activity 12, It's a Windy Day!

30 📖 Book 7 - My Cat

OBJECTIVES
1. Child will successfully read *My Cat*
2. Child will write the story line from dictation
3. Child will practice identifying questions, statements, and exclamations
4. Child will practice question marks and exclamation points.

MATERIALS

1. *My Cat* six copies
2. Sentence strips for the book text
3. Two toy cats
4. "Stocked" centers
5. Big book about a cat

ANTICIPATORY SET

Read your big book selection, making sure to read with expression. Just enjoy the story. Ask the children how many of them have a cat at home. Let them share, describing what their cat looks like if they have one.

Tell them to pretend one cat belongs to Jaylen and the other one to Marie. These children play together often with their cats. One day they were playing with their cats outside, and when it was time to go home, they forgot to take their toy cats with them! They left them in the park! Marie's older brother said he'd go look for her cat for her. He said, "Marie, what does your cat look like?" Ask the children how they would describe Marie's cat for her brother.

Jaylen's dad said he'd go look for his cat in the park. He asked, "Jaylen, what does your cat look like?" Ask the children how they would describe Jaylen's cat.

Tell the children that in today's book, a girl had a cat that she lost just like Jaylen and Marie did! She could identify her cat because of his distinct coloring.

LESSON
Read the sentence strips together after you have done your scan for good clues in reading, such as words that repeat, etc.

Review the use of punctuation and use the game from lesson 28 if desired. Although the concept of question and statement is not a difficult one for us, sometimes even second graders struggle to tell the difference between a statement and a question, so lots of practice cannot hurt!

WRITING
Follow the established routine for dictation, writing on whiteboards and board checking. If a child is having trouble with writing the correct sounds/letters, be sure he or she is sounding as each letter is written.

Again, have the children practice the formation of the punctuation marks on their whiteboards. Take a few minutes to let them write a brief question with the ? at the end. "Is it my cat?" for example.

CENTERS
Teacher Center:
Give each child at the table a copy of the book *My Cat*. Scan the book before reading it, noting the types of words, counting how many ? they find, etc.

Again, focus on moving from decoding each word to just saying the word. Review the use of two tools to help them: 1] check for what would make sense, and 2] do a quick look at the word to pick a clue, such as an initial sound or a final word family.

This time when you have finished reading the book together, practice "read and echo" in order to encourage children to read in phrases rather than one word at a time. Practice making a good stop at the end of sentences rather than running the sentences together as though there were no punctuation marks.

Reading Center:
Children will read today's book to their partner, then listen along while the other child reads. They should then spend time reading to each other books 1-6 as there is time. You will need three of each book for this center.

Scavenger Hunt:
Use the other three copies of books 1-6 and have the children search each book for their sight words. They should record what they find in their center folders. They can copy the name of the title for each book, then write the sight words they find under each title.

Journal:
Have the children write "I do not see my cat!" in their journal, then draw a picture of where the cat is hiding. Great time to use their imaginations!

This is the end of Section 1! Congratulations!
Take a few minutes to reflect on how the teaching and learning process went for your children. It would be valuable for you to take notes of how it went and what you might do differently next year. What were areas of particular difficulty? What are areas that will need to be reviewed more frequently?

Now that section 1 is over, it is time for complete assessments of each child using the Skills Tracking form. Make a photocopy for each child to send home to parents.

- Can they say the sound for each letter?
- If you say a sound, can they write the letter picture?
- Do they know all their sight words at first glance?
- Can they decode the simple 3-letter decodable words? (word family words)
- Can they read all seven books? You might want to enlist the help of a volunteer for a few days to help you listen to all the children. The volunteer could take a child at a time and listen to him/her read. You could be listening to children during teacher center as well.

Section Two Goals - Lessons 31-62

LEARNER GOALS

• The child will learn 12 more sounds and their corresponding symbols.
• The child will utilize visuals and motions in recognizing 31 new words on sight.
• The child will successfully read and re-read 8 more books.
• The child will learn the following advanced concepts:

OW & OU & OW /oh/*
S /z/*
Final LL
Final Y as /e/ and /i/*
"Pinchy E" (final "silent E")
Picture to cue reading
OU /oo/* as in YOU
Use of quotation marks
OO /oo/* as in BOOK and MOON
OR spelling pattern as in PORCH
Final S as in LIKES
Digraphs SH, CH, TH, WH
Final -ERE as in HERE, THERE, WHERE
A /ah/* as in WANT
Plurals

*/ / means "sounds like what is between slashes as in A/sounds like "ah"/

• The child will engage in comprehension activities

MATERIALS NEEDED FOR SECTION 2

• *Alphabet Tales*
• Alphabet Teaching Cards D, H, G, L, I, B, J, W, Y, N, U, R, Y
• SnapWords® cards for:
(List A, Groups 3-5, additional nouns, & "qu" words)

little	want	did	you	here
look	for	call	this	have
make	ran	as	if	hi
now	out	so	big	has
will	but	like	can	stop
get	play	down	we	said
sand	sun	ball	tree	grass
crab	quit	quick	come	

• Easy-for-Me™ Books, numbers 8-15
Dot the Tot
Jig the Pig
My Dog, Jip
I Can Hop
Do Stop
Little Dab
Bob Hums
Jip Digs
• Resources for Section 2:
(pages 143-230)

• Whiteboards, markers, and tube socks as in Section 1.

ROOM SET-UP/PREP WORK

Display the new list of sight words in a pocket chart.

Prepare all resources you will need for Section Two and have them accessible for easy retrieval on the day you will use them. This will include cutting apart the word family cards and pull-down letters.

Photocopy the Skills Tracking form found in Section 2 Resources, one copy per child. Keep these forms in a file or on a clipboard and update regularly.

WORD LISTS & WORD FAMILIES for SECTION 2

Use these words for segmenting and blending, for pull-down letters, for mixed up words, for playing Quick Draw, & for word sort activities. Add final S to increase difficulty, as in "wins."

at	ot	it	ut	ap	op	ip	am	im
hat	dot	hit	hut	gap	hop	dip	ham	dim
fat	hot	lit	gut	lap	lop	hip	bam	him
rat	got	bit	but	rap	bop	lip	jam	Jim
bat	lot	wit	jut	cap	cop	Jip	ram	rim
Nat	rot	nit	rut	map	pop	rip	yam	Tim
cat	not	sit	nut	tap	mop	yip	Sam	
sat	cot	fit	cut	sap	top	nip	Pam	

um	ad	od	id	ud	ag	og	ig	ug
hum	dad	God	did	dud	hag	dog	dig	dug
gum	had	rod	hid	bud	nag	hog	gig	hug
bum	gad	nod	lid	cud	lag	log	big	lug
rum	lad	sod	bid	mud	bag	bog	jig	bug
yum	bad	pod	rid		jag	jog	wig	jug
sum	fad	mod	Sid		wag	cog	rig	rug
	sad	cod			rag	fog	fig	mug

ab	ob	ib	ub	an	on	in	un	ill
dab	gob	bib	rub	Dan	Don	din	dun	dill
gab	lob	jib	nub	ban	Jon	bin	gun	hill
lab	bob	rib	tub	Jan	Ron	win	bun	gill
jab	job	nib	cub	ran	yon	tin	run	sill
nab	rob	fib	sub	man	con	sin	nun	Jill
tab	nob		pub	can		pin	fun	will
cab	sob			tan		fin	sun	Bill

ASSESSMENTS

Section 2 assessments will relate primarily to ongoing knowledge of sounds and their symbols, gain of fluency in decoding, blending and segmenting, and the acquisition of the sight words for this section.

If a child(ren) seems to need more practice in any of those skills, use the activities provided in Section 1 to give additional practice, and/or enlist some small group help to help the child get up to speed in these skills.

NOTES:

31 Dd

OBJECTIVES
1. Child will gain a mental visual of Dd
2. Child will use this visual to recall Dd
3. Child will connect the visual to the sound
4. Child will utilize the visual in writing Dd
5. Child will blend using Dd

MATERIALS

1. *Alphabet Tales,* page 39
2. Alphabet Teaching Card for Dd
3. Pictures of items that start with D (R53)
4. Resources 53A-54 (pp. 143-145)
5. Pictures of donuts or a couple of real
donuts to cut into bits and share with the children! See recipe for Drop Donuts in the resources section.

ANTICIPATORY SET

Ask the children how many of them like to eat donuts. Share with them your own favorite kind of donut, and then let them tell you what kind they would love to have! If you brought a donut or two, cut into little pieces and let each child have a taste.

STORY

Read the story for Dd, emphasizing the Ddd sound. Draw attention to the picture of the D's facing each other. Ask a pair of children to mimic the D's for the class, facing each other and sticking out their tummies.

VISUAL IMPRINTING

Ask the children to close their eyes and imagine seeing the D's facing each other. Point out that Dad and Don are "talking," facing each other. Their tummies almost touch, while their backs are away from each other. This might help them remember the correct formation of the letters when they are introduced to the Bb letters, as many children have difficulty distinguishing between lowercase B and D.

BODYSPELLING

uppercase D   lowercase d

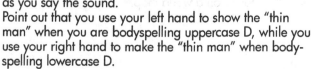

Do the motion for Dd together as you say the sound.
Point out that you use your left hand to show the "thin man" when you are bodyspelling uppercase D, while you use your right hand to make the "thin man" when bodyspelling lowercase D.

WRITING

As you say the D sound together aloud, the child(ren) will bodyspell, then practice forming the letter on their whiteboards.

The following illustrations might help if the children are having trouble remembering how to form their Dd's. Children who are right-handed will use their left hand to form a structure around which to write, while lefties will use their right hand to make the structures. Structures made will be "cave" and "point." In all cases, the thin man is drawn first.

BLENDING

This is the first lesson in which the children will have learned a sound and will blend using the sound right away. Share the objects that begin with D. Place the letter cards for A and D in your pocket chart to form a word family. Tell the children this is a new family that they will need to add to their journals, but first you are going to make some words for the family. Letter cards (R54) for T, F, C, S, M, P, and D will be used to make the words: TAD, FAD, CAD, SAD, MAD, PAD, DAD. When you blend with the word family, first time through, sound all three letters: T-A-D, but the second time through, sound like this: T-AD, D-AD, etc., in order to encourage the children to rely on what they already know about the word family as they are decoding.

CENTERS
Teacher Center:

Using the pull-down letters (R54), do initial sound replacement activities with your group. Starting with the word family AD, ask "What letter would you need to make the word TAD?" Continue on with this family of words. Other families include OT, (tot, cot, pot, dot) and OD (pod, mod, sod, cod).

Other Centers could include Journal Center to add the new letter and new word family, Books, Scavenger Hunt to find letter Ds for a class poster, Sentence Unscramble, etc.

32 Hh

OBJECTIVES
1. Child will gain a mental visual of Hh
2. Child will use this visual to recall Hh
3. Child will connect the visual to the sound
4. Child will utilize the visual in writing Hh
5. Child will blend using Hh

MATERIALS

1. *Alphabet Tales* page 43
2. Alphabet Teaching Card for Hh
3. Pictures of items that start with H (R56)
4. Resources 55-58 (pp. 146-149)
5. Pictures of castles or a story that has a castle in it
6. Plain letter cards for A, T, F, C, S, O, P, M, D, H - six each

ANTICIPATORY SET

Read your book about a castle, or share your pictures and talk briefly about what castles are, where they are found today, and then ask children what they know about castles already.

STORY

Read the story for Hh, emphasizing the breathy Hhh sound. Engage the children in a discussion about ways they would have chosen to solve the friends' problem of living so far away from each other. What would they have done? Would their solution be inventing a new contraption that would get the boys from one place to another more quickly?

VISUAL IMPRINTING

Ask the children to close their eyes and imagine seeing the two castles connected by the hanging hallway. Can they also see the castle by itself with the hallway curving to the ground? Does the hallway come out of the castle near the top? The bottom? Or near the middle? If the castle was a thin man, the hanging hallway would come out of his belly button, wouldn't it?

BODYSPELLING

uppercase H   lowercase h

Do the motion for H together and say the sound. Then do the motion for lowercase H. Point out that their left hand stays up ready to be used in either the uppercase H or the lowercase H. Only their right hand changes position.

WRITING

As you say the sound of H together aloud, the child(ren) will bodyspell, then practice forming the letter on their whiteboards.

These letters will be relatively simple for the children to form, as the children will draw two thin men with the table connecting them at their belly buttons. The lowercase H is one thin man with the curve coming out of his belly button as well, then touching the ground.

BLENDING

Share the pictures of items that begin with H (R56). Place the word family cards for AD, AT, OT, OP, AM (R55) in the pocket chart. Review what they are with the children, decoding if necessary. You will have the letter card for H as the rover in this game. First, place the H in front of AD and decode together, first saying each sound (H-A-D), and then a second time just saying the onset (H) and rime (AD) to make H-AD. Repeat this process with all the other word families. Finally, put the H in the pocket chart to the left of the column of word families and play the oral game: "Where would you put Hhh if you wanted to make HAD?" Repeat with HAT, HOP, HOT, HAM.

CENTERS

Teacher Center:
Using the pull-down letters, play a group word unscramble game. Each child will need letters for A, T, F C, S,O, P, M, D, H. Tell the children you will call out some sounds. They will need to find the pictures of those sounds and pull them down right in front of them. Then they will figure out what word they could make from those sounds. You may use the following words: PAD, HAD, HAM, DOT, HOT, SAD, FAD, HAT, TOM, MOD, SOP, MOM, POT, SOD. And non-words: POM, HOM, SOT, MOT, HOD, TOF, HOF, FOS, DOS, POS.

Illustration Center:
Give this group the R57 sheet and have them read each little sentence, then illustrate it in the box provided.

Journal Center:
This group will update their journal to include Hh and their new Hh words. They may draw the castles and the hanging bridge.

Sight Word Center:
This group will use R58.

ACROSS THE CURRICULUM
•Geography - Study castles and locate where they can still be found on a world map.

33  Gg

MATERIALS

1. *Alphabet Tales* page 47
2. Alphabet Teaching Card for Gg
3. Pictures of items that start with G (R59)
4. Resources 59-61 (pp. 150-153)
5. Pictures of gorillas or a book with a gorilla in it
6. 6 each plain cards: A, T, F, C, S,O, P, M, D, H, G

ANTICIPATORY SET

Share your gorilla book or pictures of gorillas and talk about the experiences the children have had with gorillas, either seeing them at the zoo, in books, or in TV programs. Ask the children to describe a gorilla. Is he strong? Other adjectives (describing words) could include huge, fierce-looking, powerful, etc. Share with the children that gorillas are the largest of the ape family, native to Africa, adult male weighs 500 pounds, as heavy as two and a half grown men! (See R60).

STORY

Introduce the story for Gg by sharing that in this story, the children will meet a gorilla named Gary. Tell them that after the story, you will describe Gary Gorilla and see how he compares to the gorillas you already talked about. Read the story for Gg, emphasizing the hard G sound as you do.

VISUAL IMPRINTING

Ask the children to close their eyes and imagine seeing a cave. When they are ready, say "Now, suppose you add a table to your cave so Gary has something to eat on. Can you see the table?" Then ask them to "see" Gary, or lowercase G. Which way is he looking? This memory of Gary should help the children remember later which way the hook under the G goes: **g**

BODYSPELLING

uppercase G   lowercase g

Do the motion for G together, saying the sound. Then do the motion for lowercase g. Point out that the left hand stays forming a cave, and it is the right hand that changes position.

© 2007 Sarah Major

WRITING

As you say the sound of G together aloud, the child(ren) will bodyspell, then practice forming the letter on their whiteboards.
"Starting near the top, make a large cave. Then make a little table for Gary to eat lunch on." "Make a little cave, then close up the mouth. Without lifting your marker, drop a hook down into the basement, making sure to go under the cave you made."

BLENDING

Place the word family cards for OT, AD, OD, AP, AG (R55) in the pocket chart. Review what they are with the children, decoding if necessary. You will have the letter card for G as the rover in this game.
First, place the G in front of OD and decode together, first saying each sound, (G-O-D) then a second time just saying the onset (G) and rime (OD) to make G-OD. Repeat this process with the other word families. Finally, put the G in the pocket chart to the left of the of word families and play the oral game: "Where would you put Ggg if you wanted to make GOD?" Repeat with GAD, GOT, GAP, GAG.

CENTERS

Teacher Center:
Using the pull-down cards, play the making words game as before (Lesson 32). Words you may form are: DOG, FOG, HOG, COG, TAG, SAG, HAG, GAG, SAP, TAP, CAP, MAP, GAP.
Depending on your group's readiness, you can venture into four-sound words: [TAPS, PAST] [STOP, POTS, SPOT] [MAPS, SPAM, PAMS] [SPAT, PATS, TAPS]. Say each word, use your fingers in fingermapping to help children position the sounds correctly. Have the children sound the four letter words with you as you point to the corresponding fingers, then have them sound as they put the letters together. Notice that there are only four groups of letters, but more than one word for each group.

Little Book Center:
Use R60 as a basis for studying gorillas and let the children make little books with their gorilla facts.

Journal Center:
This group will update their journal to include Gg and their new Gg words.

Sight Word Center:
This group will take R61, cut the sentences off the bottom and then glue each sentence under the picture that best illustrates it.

ACROSS THE CURRICULUM
• Science - Study gorillas.

34 now*

OBJECTIVES
1. Child will review word wall words & new words
2. Child will learn sight word NOW
3. Child will find NOW in print
4. Child will use sight word in sentences

MATERIALS

1. SnapWords® List A Group 2 displayed
2. Yellow crayons (6)
3. SnapWords® List A Group 3
4. Plain letter cards for C, S, P, H, T, M, D, F
5. OW on a plain card (see R54, p. 145)
6. Resources 62-65 (pp. 154-157)

ANTICIPATORY SET

Gather the children around you and the List A Group 2 SnapWords® in the pocket chart (it, sit, to, up, or, help, I, my, see, now, do, he, now). Arrange the words like this: "NOW I SIT..." and let the children read the phrase with you and then fill in the blank with they sit on or by. You may choose to use the bean bag to toss to a child who will take a turn making a sentence that starts with those words. He then will toss the bean bag to another child. Additional sentence starters are: "NOW I HELP MY...", "NOW I SEE MY..."

LESSON - Sight Word NOW

Warm up by playing **Pop Up** for a few minutes. Alternative games are activities 4 & 5, Around the World and Which is Which?

When you are ready to focus on today's new sound spelling (OW) and the word NOW, share the visual (R62) with the children. Explore the pictures of OW and OW (pronounced OH). Point out that the picture of the sounds look exactly alike, but there are two different sounds that have the same picture. Place the card with OW written on it in the pocket chart. Next place the letter cards in a column on the left of the OW card. Tell the children you are going to investigate which four letter pictures will blend with OW to make a real word. Take turns placing a letter in front of OW and decoding. The words that can be formed are: COW, SOW, POW, AND HOW.

WRITING

Because today is the end of List A, Group 2, practice finding and writing the plain words using word wall words, or the reverse side of the stylized cards. You will say, "Find and write NOW." Children will write on their whiteboards. Continue like this, doing quick visual checks, until all the Group 2 words have been located and written.

Play Activity 11 from Activities for Use with SnapWords® - Oral Sentence-Building. (p. 283)

Next, play Activity 9 - Word Flip until all the words are turned over. (p. 283)

GRADUATION!

Tell the children that today is the day you will "graduate" Group 2 words to the classroom word wall. Make a big deal out of posting the plain green word wall words to the wall while the children are watching. Next, take out List A, Group 3 words and place them one at a time in the pocket chart as you briefly introduce each word as detailed in Activity 1 in Appendix A.

CENTERS

Teacher Center:

Use R63 to highlight the OW sound spelling in unknown words. You will read the word under each picture and ask the children if they can find the OW picture in each word. They don't have to be able to read the words in order to do this activity with you. They will locate the OW spellings and color them with a yellow crayon.

Use R64 to follow up your lesson about OW and OW. This resource will have eight pictures. Say the word that goes with each picture with the children, then do the auditory discrimination activity: Have the children sort the picture cards into two groups based on whether the OW sounds like OW or OH. Go over the results together.

Pocket Chart Center:

Making sentences with sight words to write in center folders.

Scavenger Hunt:

Children will look for NOW in print, cut them out and glue on paper, or highlight them with a yellow crayon.

Sentence Unscramble:

Same procedure as before. Use R65.

35 OUT, SO

OBJECTIVES
1. Child will review word wall words & new words
2. Child will learn sight words OUT, GO
3. Child will find OUT, GO in print
4. Child will use sight words in sentences

MATERIALS

1. SnapWords® List A Group 3 displayed
2. Resource 62
3. Old newspapers or magazines
4. Plain letter cards for C, S, P, H, T, M, D, F
5. OW & OU on plain cards
6. Resources 66-68 (pp. 158-160)

ANTICIPATORY SET

Gather the children around you and the List A Group 3 SnapWords in the pocket chart. Review Activity 1 from yesterday, seeing if the children can take the lead in telling you what each word says before you just tell them. Ask them to share with you which is their favorite word and why. They might want to take turns using a sight word in a short sentence orally.

LESSON - Sight Words OUT & SO
Show the children the sight word OUT. Have them say it. Ask them if they hear the OU sound in OUT. Ask them if they remember learning that sound recently. Wait to see if a child connects the sound of OU in OUT to the sound of OW in NOW. If they do not make this connection for themselves, prompt them to listen for OU with their eyes closed. Ask them to give you a thumbs up if they hear that sound. Say: "OUT, GO, COW, CLOUD, HORSE, TREE, BROWN, TOWEL." Praise them for good listening!

Share with the children the visual on Resource 62. Talk about how we might cry "Ow!" when we fall down and get hurt. Show that the wide open mouth of the Ow and Ou are to remind them of the sound of these "bandaid" spellings. Now use R66. Say, "Many times, we use OW at the end of words like a caboose on a train, while we use OU in the middle of words like the baloney in a sandwich. Most often the only letter appearing after OW is N." N is pretty strong and is very often the only letter strong enough to follow OW!

Display SO and ask the children if there are other words they have learned recently that rhyme with it. (NO and GO). Review the fact that TO and DO look the same but sound very different!

WRITING

Show the children their new sight words one at a time. Let them look/study the word for a few seconds, then they should look down and write what they saw without looking up again. If they forget the sequence of O and U in OUT, use the phrase "OH YOU must be joking!" to help them remember that O comes before U. When they write SO, ask them to also write NO and GO under SO.

CENTERS
Teacher Center:

Use R67 with your groups. They will first color the OU and OW they find in the word bank words, then they will cut out the words. They will need to sort the words under the correct picture target at the top of the sheet.

Pocket Chart Center:
Making sentences with sight words to write in center folders. Be sure to include the new sight words.

Scavenger Hunt:
Children will look for words containing either OU or OW and will cut them out to share with their group when they are with the teacher. The group that met with the teacher first will get to share the next day.

Word Search:
Use R68 and let the children search for their Group 2 sight words.

Assessments:
Using the Skill Tracking form for Section Two, begin doing assessments on sounds and sight words for each child. Make additional notes to yourself as you notice any area that might need strengthening in each child.

36   Ll

OBJECTIVES
1. Child will gain a mental visual of Ll
2. Child will use this visual to recall Ll
3. Child will connect the visual to the sound
4. Child will utilize the visual in writing Ll
5. Child will blend using Ll

MATERIALS

1. *Alphabet Tales*, page 51
2. Alphabet Teaching Card for Ll
3. Pictures of items that start with L (R69)
4. Resources 69-71 (pp. 161-163)
5. The biggest pair of shoes you can find
6. 6 each letter cards: A, T, F, C, S,O, P, M, D, H, G, L

ANTICIPATORY SET

Show the children your huge pair of shoes and let them comment about them. Ask if they ever tried on some shoes that were really big. How did it feel? Ask them what it would be like if we didn't have any feet. What are our feet for (besides walking on!)? Let the children stand up and practice leaning forward a bit. What holds them up and keeps them from falling? Their feet do! Our feet keep us from tipping over. Our story today is about a little boy named Larry who kept on tipping over!

STORY

Read the story for Ll and emphasize the Lll sound in the story.
When you have finished, let the children reflect to you what they might have done had they been asked to help poor Larry stop tipping over. Let them share for a few minutes.

VISUAL IMPRINTING

Ask the children to close their eyes and imagine seeing little Larry before he got his lovely lavender shoes. What does he look like? A pencil? A thin man? What does he look like with his lavender shoes? Which way is he looking? (to the right at his brother). Ask the children to keep their eyes closed and draw Larry in the air.

BODYSPELLING

uppercase L   lowercase l

Do the motion for L together, saying the sound. Then do the motion for lowercase l. L is fun because you just make a thin man with your hand, then for uppercase L, you stick out your thumb! So easy!

WRITING

As you say the sound for L together aloud, the child(ren) will bodyspell, then practice forming the letter on their whiteboards.
Lowercase L obviously, is just a thin man with no feet or anything! Uppercase L is Larry after he got his lovely lavender shoes. Children will draw the thin man, stop at the bottom line, then turn a sharp corner and draw the table right along the bottom line.

BLENDING
Share the pictures of items that begin with L. Place the word family cards for OT, AD, OP, AP, AG, OG (R71) in the pocket chart. Review what they are with the children, decoding if necessary. You will have the letter card for L as the rover in this game. First, place the L in front of AD and decode together, first saying each sound, (L-A-D) then a second time just saying the onset (L) and rime (AD) to make L-AD. Repeat this process with the other word families. Finally, put the L in the pocket chart to the left of the of word families and play the oral game: "Where would you put Llll if you wanted to make LAD?" Repeat with LOT, LAP, LOP, LAG, LOG.

CENTERS
Teacher Center:
Using the pull-down letters, play the making words game as before (Lesson 32). Words you may form are: SAL, PAL, HAL, CAL, GAL. Depending on your group's readiness, you can practice using four-sound words: Say, "Find Aa, Ll, Tt, & Ss." When each child has his four letters in front of him, say, "The word is LAST. Sound it with me. L-A-S-T. Now, put your sound pictures in the right order so that you make the word LAST." Have the children sound as they find the right letters. When they have put the letters in the right order, say, "Now that you have made LAST, please take the Aa away. Now find a sound to put in its place so the word will say LOST. L-O-S-T." Have the children sound O while they are searching for the letter. Repeat this activity in making FAST, then changing it to MAST. TAPS-TOPS, TOPS-COPS, COPS-COTS, COTS-CATS, CATS-CAPS, CAPS-MAPS. Other words to use: SLAP, SLAT, PLAT, GLAD, SLOP, PLOP, CLAP.

Journal Center:
This group will update their journal to include Ll and their new Ll words. They may draw Little Larry and his brother.

Other Centers:
Depending on what you think your class needs, choose centers that will reinforce or provide more practice in those areas. Use R70 for word unscramble if desired.

37 Book 8 - Dot the Tot

```
OBJECTIVES
1. Child will successfully read Dot the Tot
2. Child will write the story line from dictation
3. Child will correctly sequence events in the story
```

MATERIALS

1. *Dot the Tot*, six copies
2. Sentence strips for the book text
3. Resources 72-73 (pp. 164-165)
4. "Stocked" centers

ANTICIPATORY SET

Ask your students how many of them have a younger brother or sister at home. Let them have time to respond. Remind the children that sometimes we use the word TOT to talk about a child who is not a baby, but who is not really big either. There was such a child in the third book they read (*Tot in a Cot*). Tell them that their story for today is about a little girl named Dot who got really hot while she was taking a nap in her cot. Ask the children if they have ever gotten very warm while they were sleeping under a blanket. What might be some ways they chose to cool off?

LESSON

Read the sentence strips together after you have done your scan for good clues in reading, such as words that repeat, etc. Do a search for the family OT that repeats frequently throughout the story. Review the use of an exclamation point. Encourage the students as they read to not decode the OT words, but just add the initial sound to OT.

WRITING

Follow the established routine for dictation, writing on whiteboards and board checking. If a child is having trouble with writing the correct sounds/letters, be sure he or she is sounding audibly as each letter is written.

Dictate short phrases from the book and check for problems.

CENTERS

Teacher Center:
Give each child at the table a copy of the book *Dot the Tot*. Scan the book before reading it, noting the OT words. If possible, let each child have a turn to read the story, but if there is not enough time, have the children take turns reading pages.

Reading Center:
Children will read today's book to their partner, then listen along while the other child reads. They should then spend time reading to each other books 1-7 as there is time. You will need three of each book for this center.

Picture/Phrase Match-up:
Use R73 and have children cut out the sentences and glue them under the picture that best matches the sentence. This activity will give them practice in both reading and comprehension.

Journal:
Have the children write about *Dot the Tot* in their journal, then draw a picture of what Dot did when she got really hot in her cot!

Word Family Sort:
A center idea is to give the children index cards on which are words from 2-3 families of words. Don't tell them how to sort the cards, just that they have to be grouped in families. The group must come to an agreement on their own as to how to sort the words. They should record their groups in their center folders for you to review later.
Word ideas are:
DOT, TOT, HOT, GOT, LOT
DAD, HAD, GAD, LAD, BAD
DOG, HOG, LOG, BOG, JOG

ACROSS THE CURRICULUM
• Science ~ Use R72 for hot and cold sort.

38 Ii

OBJECTIVES
1. Child will gain a mental visual of Ii
2. Child will use this visual to recall Ii
3. Child will connect the visual to the sound
4. Child will utilize the visual in writing Ii
5. Child will blend using Ii

MATERIALS

1. *Alphabet Tales,* page 55
2. Alphabet Teaching Card for Ii
3. Pictures of items that start with Ii (R74)
4. Resources 71, 74-76 (pp. 163, 166-168
5. A picture book showing the life of Plains Indians or other Native Americans.
6. 6 each letter cards: T, F, S, P, M, D, H, G, L, I

ANTICIPATORY SET

Share with the children your book and talk about some of their customs, the Native American community and how each member in the community contributed to life for the group, the buffalo hunts, their dress, and their respect and care for the world and nature (if about the Plains Indians).

STORY

Read the story for Ii and point out to them that the uppercase I is like the word I they use when they talk about themselves. You should at this point, however, emphasize the short sound of I (i, as in igloo).

VISUAL IMPRINTING

Ask the children to close their eyes and imagine seeing little Ichabod and Ivan as they stood. They might want to make their whole body be an uppercase I by pointing their toes out and stretching out their arms.

BODYSPELLING

uppercase I   lowercase i

Do the motion for Ii together, saying the sound. Then do the motion for lowercase i. Make sure everyone is saying a short, staccato type of sound for short Ii.

WRITING

Spend a few minutes saying the sound of Ii and as you say the sound together aloud, the child(ren) will bodyspell, then practice forming the letter on their whiteboards.

It would be a great time to review with your students the proper use of an uppercase letter - for starting a sentence, for starting a person's name, and all by itself when speaking of yourself.

BLENDING

Place the word family cards for IT, ID, IP, IG (R71), in the pocket chart. Review what they are with the children, decoding if necessary. The game is different this time because of the central position of the short Ii sound. Hold up three fingers and show the children the position the Ii will have by pointing to your middle finger. Tell them to watch carefully for the Ii as you build words. To the left of your column of rimes, place the letters T, F, S, P, M, D, H, G, L. For the IT family, you can make: HIT, LIT, PIT, SIT, FIT. For the ID family you can make: DID, HID, LID, SID, MID. For the IP family, make: DIP, TIP, SIP, HIP, LIP. For IG, make: DIG, GIG, PIG, FIG. After you have done this exercise orally with the children, play Quick Draw, using the format detailed on page 9 of this manual. Use the same words you did orally for this game.

CENTERS
Teacher Center:

Share pictures of items beginning with I. Using the pull-down letters, play the making words game as before (Lesson 32). Words you may form are above. For your advanced group, or as you feel all groups may be ready, use the following four letter words. Go slowly enough that all children can be successful, use your fingermapping to show children where letter sounds fall, and make sure they sound both with you before they start, and as they are putting their letters into order.

Four-letter words to use: SIPS, SIFT, LIPS, FLIT, SLIT, FITS-FIST, PITS-SPIT, DIPS, RIFT, LIST, and bonus word SPLIT. (*when sounding blends such as SP, say each sound separately. Even in blends you can hear two distinct sounds and so when segmenting, each sound must be pronounced separately. SPIT would be segmented: S-P-I-T, not SP-I-T.)

Journal Center:
This group will update their journal to include the new word families and their Ii words.

Picture/Sentence Match:
Use R75 for this center.

Sight Words Search:
Use R76 for this center.

ACROSS THE CURRICULUM
•Social Studies - Study a Native American tribe and their contribution to our country. See http://www.saskschools.ca/~gregory/firstnations/index.html
•Art - Research symbols used in the tribe you have chosen, and let the children reproduce them.

39   Jj

OBJECTIVES
1. Child will gain a mental visual of Jj
2. Child will use this visual to recall Jj
3. Child will connect the visual to the sound
4. Child will utilize the visual in writing Jj
5. Child will blend using Jj

MATERIALS

1. *Alphabet Tales*, page 59
2. Alphabet Teaching Card for Jj
3. Pictures of junk, or a book about recycling
4. Pictures of items that start with Jj (R77)
5. Resources 71, 77-79 (pp. 163, 169-171)
7. 6 each letter cards: J, P, M, G, O, A, I, H, T, C, F

ANTicipatory SET

Share with the children your book about recycling - the idea is to focus on making something new and useful out of what we might think is junk. Discuss what happens when people throw junk into our rivers and lakes. The harm to sea life, the polution of our water, etc. Ask how many of them have ever gone fishing and snagged something on their hook that was not a fish?

STORY

Introduce the story for Jj by telling the children that in this story, a lot of people were taking junk and making new things out of it. Read the story for Jj focusing on the sound of the letter.

VISUAL IMPRINTING

Ask the children to close their eyes and imagine seeing the Jollys' sign. Ask them which way the hook on the J goes. Many children reverse the letter J, so we will be offering visual helps to help prevent reversals.

BODYSPELLING

Do the motion for J together, using your right hands, and saying the sound. Then do the motion for lowercase j. The sound for Jj is a short sound, not JUH, which is really two sounds: J and short sound for U.

uppercase J   lowercase j

WRITING
Spend a few minutes saying the sound of Jj. As you say the sound together aloud, the child(ren) will bodyspell, then practice forming the letter on their whiteboards.
Use R78 to show children the direction for J.

If they don't make the hook on the J going the right way, they could pop the next letter with the sharp point on the hook of the J.

BLENDING

Share the pictures of items that begin with J. Place the word family cards for IP, AG, OG, IG (R71) in the pocket chart. You will also use single letter cards A & M to make AM, and I & M to make IM. The letter J is placed to the left of your column of word families. Practice blending with J as the onset as you have done in previous lessons. Words you will make are: JIP, JAM, JIM, JAG, JOG, JIG. After you have done this exercise orally with the children, play Quick Draw, using the format detailed on page 9 of this manual. Use the same words you did orally for this game. Next, add some four letter words, offering plenty of support as you do: JIGS, JAMS, JOGS, JAGS, JIMS.

Next, tell the children they will be listening for vowels A, O, I (say their short sounds). You will say each word, and the children will respond by bodyspelling the letter sound they hear, A, O, or I. (Words used are: MAT, FIG, POT, DOG, BAT, COT, CAP, HOT, HAT, HIT, JAM, JOG.)

CENTERS
Teacher Center:

Using the pull-down letters, you will play a game with your group. Start by asking them to spell PIG with their letters. When everyone has PIG, tell them to take one letter off so they can make PIT. Offer enough support by segmenting (P-I-T) so the children will select the correct letter to replace. If your group is not able to do this well yet, start by asking them which letter they would need to take off PIG if they wanted to make PIT. Next:
- PIT to PAT
- PAT to HAT
- HAT to HOT
- HOT to POT
- POT to COT
- COT to CAT
- CAT to FAT
- FAT to FIT

Journal Center:
This group will update their journal to include their J words.

Sentence Illustrate:
Use R79 for this center.

Pocket Chart:
Use sight words in pocket chart to make sentences.

ACROSS THE CURRICULUM
- Social Studies - Recycling would be a very worthwhile topic to study with your children.
- Art - Bring in found objects and see what your children can create if they glue them on paper to make a collage.

 **40**  Bb big

do to help themselves keep b and d straight.

OBJECTIVES
1. Child will gain a mental visual of Bb
2. Child will use this visual to recall Bb
3. Child will utilize the visual in writing Bb
4. Child will blend using Bb
5. Child will learn BIG

MATERIALS

1. *Alphabet Tales*, page 63
2. Alphabet Teaching Card for Bb
3. Story book or picture book about bears
4. Pictures of items that start with Bb (R80)
5. Resources 80-84 (pp. 172-176)
6. SnapWords® Card for BIG
7. 6 each letter cards: T, P, D, G, B, I, O, A, S

ANTICIPATORY SET

Ask the children if they have seen a bear and what all they know about bears. After they have shared for a few minutes, share your story or book on bears.

STORY

Introduce the story for Bb by telling the children that you are going to have a story about some very special bears. These bears could TALK, and they did not hibernate!
Read the story of Bb and emphasize the Bb sound as you read.

VISUAL IMPRINTING

Ask the children to close their eyes and imagine seeing the bears as they are walking. Which way do their tummies point as they are walking? Are their tummies pointing the same direction? Or are they facing each other like the Dee's were?

BODYSPELLING

Do the motion for B together, pointing out that they will make the thin man with their left hands for both uppercase and lowercase B. Their right hand is the only one that changes what it does.

uppercase B   lowercase b

WRITING

As you say the sound of B together aloud, the child(ren) will bodyspell, then practice forming the letter on their whiteboards.
Use R82 to show the children what they can

BLENDING & SIGHT WORD - BIG

Share the pictures of items that begin with Bb. Place the word family cards for AT, IT, OP, AM, AD, ID, AG, OG, IG, OB in the pocket chart. (R83) The letter B is placed to the left of your column of word families. Practice blending with B as the onset as you have done in previous lessons. Words you will make are: BAT, BIT, BOP, BAM, BAD, BID, BAG, BOG, BIG, BOB. After you have done this exercise orally with the children, play QUICK DRAW. Use the same words you did orally for this game. Next, add some four letter words, offering plenty of support as you do: BATS, STAB, BAGS, BOGS, BOPS. Be sure children are audibly sounding as they write words on their whiteboards. Briefly introduce the sight word BIG using the stylized card.

Next, introduce an auditory game to the children. You will say a word. They will bodyspell the VOWEL they hear in the middle. Then you will change the word and they will bodyspell the new vowel. Use these words: CAT - COT, TAP-TIP, MOP-MAP, FAT-FIT, DOG-DIG, MAT-MIT, TIM-TOM.

CENTERS
Teacher Center:

Write the following words on a whiteboard, or make them with letters in a pocket chart: PIG, PAT, SAD, SOD, DID, POP. Make them in a column. Tell your students that they are going to play a game with you in which they take one word at a time and switch just one letter for a B. They will have to think and be detectives to come up with the right letter to switch with a B. Talk through the first word together. Start with PIG. Which letter can you take off and replace with a B? Should we take off the G? We would have PIB. Hmmm is that a word? Can we take off the I and change it to a B? We would have PBG. That is most certainly not a word! Continue in this way if they need the support, but if they can do this exercise on their own, let them. (PIG-BIG, PAT-BAT, SAD-BAD, SOD-SOB, DID-BID, POP-BOP) Use R81 as an activity to distinguish B and D.

Journal Center:
This group will update their journal to include their B words.

Word Families:
Use R84 for this center. Children will have two word families and will cut out the onset letters. They will hold each letter by the AB word family to see how many of them form words, then by the OB, then IB word families.

Pocket Chart:
Use sight words in pocket chart to make sentences.

ACROSS THE CURRICULUM
•**Geography** - Discover what kinds of bears live in various parts of the world.
•**Science** - Tie in your emphasis on bears with the study of hibernation.

41  has

MATERIALS

1. SnapWords® List A, Group 3 displayed
2. 2 objects, same but with different characteristics (ie 2 stuffed cats, not alike)
3. Old magazines & newspapers
4. Class names on cards, two sets
5. Resources 85-87 (pp. 177-179)

ANTICIPATORY SET

Gather the children around you and the List A Group 3 SnapWords® in the pocket chart. Review Activity 1 p. 282, seeing if the children can take the lead in telling you what each word says. Draw attention to the word HAS. Show the class your two cats (or the other objects you brought). Say, "I have two cats here and they don't look anything alike, do they?" Select two children to stand in front of the group. Give each child a cat. Then say, "Aneesha HAS a white cat. It is big." Repeat with the second child. Draw attention to the new sight word and hold it up as you repeat the sentences you just said.

LESSON - Sight Word HAS

On your whiteboard, write the words IS and AS nice and big. Ask the children to read IS first. Then ask them to change the starting sound and read AS. Point out that the S doesn't sound soft like Spotty Snake, but rather it makes a hard fizzing noise. It might tickle their tongues when they say IS or AS. Next hold up an H card in front of IS. Sound together, then repeat with AS. Show the children how you can use these two words together: "Nick HAS HIS white cat." Play a quick oral game by tossing a beanbag to a child. He is to select another student and quickly say what that student HAS. "Rick HAS blue pants on." He would toss the bean bag to Rick who would repeat the process with another child.

WRITING

Show the children their new sight word, let them study the word for a few seconds, then they should look down and write what they saw without looking up again. An easy prompt for those who forget is to ask them to sound out the word H-A-[fizzy S]. Practice dictating short sentences for them to write on their whiteboards. "Sam has a bat." "Pat has a cat." "Matt has a bat." "Pam has a cap." Ask the children to sound out the words they write, a letter at a time.

Tell the children that during their writing center, they will be designing a page to go into a class book. Each child will make one page. There are lines on which they will write their sentences, and a box in which to draw their picture. They will need a word bank of the class members' names. You could write the children's names on cards. When a group goes to the writing center, they would draw one name card out of the basket and that would be who they write about. On their sheet R85 they will find a word bank of objects they may use if they would like to. They are to write "[name] has a [object]. It is [big, a color]." Use all the pages to make a class book.

CENTERS
Teacher Center:

Use R86 with your groups. Practice reading the little story. Let the children take turns reading. Let the children illustrate the stories in the boxes provided. Use this time to do individual assessments, using the Skills Tracking form for Section 2.

Pocket Chart Center:
Making sentences with sight words to write in center folders. Use the word HAS along with their current sight words and the name cards of class members. You also could make available color words on cards.

Scavenger Hunt:
Children will look for the word HAS in print. If they glue their HAS to a paper, they could form their sentence around it rather than writing HAS for themselves.

Words in Big Words:
Use R87 and let the children search for their Group 3 sight words.

LOOKING AHEAD
This lesson marks the beginning of the practice of daily journal writing. Each day, the children will write 1-3 sentences in their journals and draw a picture of what they wrote. Some children have no problems with doing this, but others, maybe the more visual, need to draw their picture first and write afterwards.

Reviewing the children's writing is vital in helping you know where they are, what concepts need to be taught, where their interest lies in terms of words they will want to use in their writing. Invest the time to go over the journals, taking notes for yourself of the errors made in spelling so that you can teach these concepts. It is very important to note that if you teach what the children are wanting to write, they will learn far more than if you teach only what your manual says you should teach next.

 **Ww**  **will**

OBJECTIVES
1. Child will gain a mental visual of Ww
2. Child will use this visual to recall Ww
3. Child will connect the visual to the sound
4. Child will utilize the visual in writing Ww
5. Child will blend using Ww
6. Child will read and write sight word WILL

MATERIALS

1. *Alphabet Tales*, page 67
2. Alphabet Teaching Card for Ww
3. Picture book about walruses
4. Pictures of items that start with Ww (R88)
5. Resources 88-90 (pp. 180-182)
6. SnapWords® Card for WILL
7. Letter cards: D, H, G, S, J, W, word family ILL

ANTICIPATORY SET

Ask the children if they have seen a walrus and what they know about them. After they have shared for a few minutes, share your story or book on walruses. Ask the children what they notice first on a walrus, using good describing words. Just before reading the story, ask the children if they had ever wanted something really badly, so that they tried to do something about it, but they ended up worse off? Tell them our story for today is how this very thing happened to two walruses!

STORY

Read the story for Ww, emphasizing the sounds of Ww. Let the children reflect after the story about what the walruses did in order to spend more time with the children. What might have been a better plan for them to make?

VISUAL IMPRINTING

Ask the children to close their eyes and imagine seeing the walruses. With their eyes closed, have the children form a W in the air with their fingers. Prompt them to start at the top and go down first.

BODYSPELLING

uppercase and lowercase W

Do the motion for W together, saying, "wrists and thumbs together, fingers spread out like wings." You can use the same motion for uppercase and lowercase W, as they are formed the same way.

WRITING

As you say the sound of Ww together aloud, the child(ren) will bodyspell, then practice forming the letter on their whiteboards.

Dictate these words for the children to write on their whiteboards: WAG, WIT, WIG. Dictate also WAG IS BIG. THE PIG HAS A WIG. MY DOG IS WAG.

BLENDING & SIGHT WORD - WILL

Place the word family cards for IT, AG, IG, ILL in the pocket chart. The letter W is placed to the left of your column of word families. Practice blending with W as the onset as you have done in previous lessons. Words you will make are: WIT, WAG, WIG, WILL.

Next, introduce the sight word WILL to the children, pointing out that the ending has two LL's. Tell the children that both LL's together say one sound, and that they will find the double LL in many words in books. Place the word family ILL in the pocket chart and use letters: D, H, G, S, J, W for onsets. Blend each word with the class.

CENTERS
Teacher Center:

Share R88. Use R89 with the children. They will each have one baggie, will empty their words onto the table, then figure out what their sentence says. The children should take turns reading their sentence to the group. Let them collaborate in forming new sentences using the words they have. After the first center, start asking the children who have come from journaling to share their writing with the group. Make notes for yourself about teaching opportunities. From now on, review journals with the groups as they come to you before continuing on with your lesson.

Journal Center:
This group will update their journal to include their W words. Next they will choose a topic to write about, write at least one good sentence, then illustrate their writing.

Which vowel?
Use R90 for this center. Children will need to write the word that corresponds to the picture. Focus is on correct vowels especially.

Pocket Chart:
Use sight words in pocket chart to make sentences.

ACROSS THE CURRICULUM
•Art - Ask the children to make big W's and draw a walrus around it. Make sure they draw fish for the walrus to eat! (See Alphabet Teaching Card, reverse side)
•Science - Study walruses. Expand the study if you like to include other animals that live in cold climates.

43   Rr

OBJECTIVES
1. Child will gain a mental visual of Rr
2. Child will use this visual to recall Rr
3. Child will connect the visual to the sound
4. Child will utilize the visual in writing Rr
5. Child will blend using Rr

MATERIALS

1. *Alphabet Tales*, page 71
2. Alphabet Teaching Card for Rr
3. Picture book about a runner in a race
4. Pictures of items that start with Rr (R91)
5. Resources 91-93 (pp. 183-184, 189)
6. Pair of running shoes

ANTICIPATORY SET

Show the children your running shoes and let them describe them (lightweight, colors, rubber soles). Ask them if they have running shoes, and if so, what do their shoes look like? Do they help you run faster? Share your book about a runner and a race.

STORY

Read the story for Rr and emphasize the sound for R as you do. Let the children comment at the end about Rebecca's problem with forgetting where she was going.

VISUAL IMPRINTING

Ask the children to close their eyes and imagine seeing Rebecca at the starting line-up, ready to take off on her race. After the children open their eyes, have them stand up and make an R with their bodies like Rebecca did.

BODYSPELLING

Do the motion for R together, pointing out that they will primarily be using their left hands to make the letters. Their right hand will make Rebecca's back leg for the uppercase letter.

uppercase R   lowercase r

WRITING

As you say the sound of Rr together aloud, the child(ren) will bodyspell, then practice forming the letter on their whiteboards.
Dictate these words for the children to write on their whiteboards: RAM, ROT, RIG, RAP, RIP, ROD, RAT. Then dictate a few short sentences for them to sound and write: RON HAS A RIG. A RAT IS BY ROB.

BLENDING

Share R91. Place the word family cards in your pocket chart (R92). Use R as the roving card that will provide the onset for the words. Blend with the children these words: RAT, ROT, RAP, RIP, RAM, RIM, ROD, RID, RIG, ROB, RIB. (also R83)
After oral blending do an auditory practice game. Say the words below and ask the children to identify the middle vowel by bodyspelling the vowel sound they hear in each word: RAG, RIG, TOP, TIP, TAP, SIP, RAT, RIP, TAP, TIP, TOP.
Next, you will toss a bean bag and have the child who catches it tell you a word with A in the middle. Keep to this vowel for a couple more times, then switch to O words, and finally do I words.

CENTERS
Teacher Center:
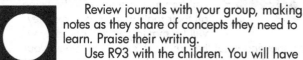
Review journals with your group, making notes as they share of concepts they need to learn. Praise their writing.
Use R93 with the children. You will have cut the sheet into strips and the children will take turns reading one strip. As time permits, assign a new strip to each child. These sentences will review all the sight words they have learned to date (29).

Journal Center:
This group will update their journal to include their Rr words. Next they will choose a topic to write about, write at least one good sentence, then illustrate their writing.

Reading Center:
Children will read alone or to a partner.

Pocket Chart:
Use sight words in pocket chart to make sentences.

LOOKING AHEAD
Lesson 44 is a review day in centers. Depending on how it goes, plan to do some updating on your Skills Tracking form.

ACROSS THE CURRICULUM
•Health - Study the importance of exercise and fresh air to our health.

44

OBJECTIVES
1. Child will review 17 letter sounds
2. Child will practice blending & segmenting
3. Child will review 29 sight words
4. Child will read using their sounds & sight words

MATERIALS

1. SnapWords® learned to date
2. Copies of the 8 books read to date
3. Resources 94-98 (pp. 185-187, 190-193)
4. Skills Tracking form
5. Stocked centers

ANTicipatory SET
Introduce this lesson by telling the children they are going to be using all their tools in their toolbox, they will be making words, and they will be showing what they know. It is good to review your expectations for how the children will move from center to center, and assign a child to be group leader. What follows are options for centers, depending on what works best for your class.

WHOLE GROUP REVIEW/Assessment:
Add OUT, SO, BIG, HAS, WILL to the word wall before you do this activity. Children will have their whiteboards, but will write on paper so you can collect and check:

OPPOSITES
1. Find the word that is the opposite of you (ME).
2. Find a word that is opposite of "away from" (BY).
3. Find the word that is the opposite of in (OUT).
4. Find the opposite of yes (NO).
5. Find the opposite of down (UP).
6. Find the opposite of she (HE).
7. Find the opposite of stand (SIT).
8. Find the opposite of later (NOW).
9. Find the opposite of little (BIG).
10. Find the opposite of come (GO).
11. Find the opposite of won't (WILL).
12. Find the opposite of your (MY).

RHYMING
1. Find a word that rhymes with hat (AT).
2. That rhymes with fizz (IS).
3. That rhymes with fin (IN).
4. That rhymes with hi (MY, I).
5. That rhymes with yelp (HELP).
6. That rhymes with store (OR).
7. That rhymes with free (HE, SEE).
8. That rhymes with shot (NOT).
9. That rhymes with Don (ON).
10. That rhymes with to (DO).

CENTERS
Fill-in-the-Blank:

Use R95, which is a sheet with familiar lines from their book seven. The children will need to read the sentences and write in the missing word. If you prefer that some children work with a partner, each child should still write his or her own words.

Bingo Center:
Use R96 and either assign a reliable group leader to call words from cards, or use a helper. This will be a sight word review.

Making Words:
Use R97, cut apart and put into baggies. The children will need to each choose a bag, put the word together, write it in their center folders, then pass the bag to their neighbor. Bags should circulate around the table.

Sentence/ Picture Match:
Use R98. Children will cut the sentences off the bottom of the sheet and glue them where they belong. The sentences each will go with a picture.
This activity will test comprehension.

More:
For students who are advanced: Provide them with letter cards and sight words. Have them:
1. Form as many words as they can with the letters, writing the words down on blank cards.
2. Create sentences using their word cards.

Teacher Center:
Use this time to do **assessments**. If you have a whole group at your table, assess **sight word recognition** by having the children face your pocket chart in which you have placed plain versions of all 29 sight words learned to date. Say "Find and write [word]." If you read the assessment from a list you keep, it will make checking easier. Use R94 for sounds assessment in game format.

Assess sounds two ways: First, go through the list of sounds they know, saying a sound and giving the children time to write the corresponding picture on their papers. You say "aaa" and they write A, etc.

Next, use the Lily Pad games and have the children cover the sounds they hear you say with little frogs. Dictate a sentence or two: "The dog is by the hog." "The pig is big." "The pig has a wig." "Wag is a rat." Check their writing for accuracy.

OBJECTIVES
1. Child will successfully read *Jig the Pig*
2. Child will write the story line from dictation
3. Child will correctly sequence events in the story

MATERIALS

1. *Jig the Pig*, six copies
2. Sentence strips for the book text
3. Resources 99-100 (pp. 194-195)
4. Stocked centers
5. Three Little Pigs book if desired

ANTICIPATORY SET

 Read the story of the Three Little Pigs to the class if desired. Otherwise remind them of this story, reviewing it a bit or asking the children to tell you what happened in the story. Tell them that today you are going to learn more about one of the three pigs that went out into the world to build a house and seek his fortune. This pig's name was Jig. Jig the Pig.

LESSON

Before you read the sentence strips, introduce the new vocabulary that will appear in this book: WIG, RIG, FIG. Use R99 for this purpose. Read together after you have done your scan for good clues in reading, such as words that repeat, etc. Do a search for the family IG that repeats frequently throughout the story. Remind the children that when they see any IG's, they can just say IG instead of sounding it out I-G. Read the strips to the children first, then have them choral read with you. Tell the children that you need every voice reading to prevent some children from doing the reading for the whole group.

WRITING

Follow the established routine for dictation, writing on whiteboards and board checking. If a child is having trouble with writing the correct sounds/letters, be sure he or she is sounding as each letter is written.

Dictate little sentences such as "Jig is a big pig." "Jig the pig has a wig." "Jig the pig has a figs."

CENTERS
Teacher Center:

Give each child at the table a copy of the book *Jig the Pig*. Read the cover, then title page, then move to page two. Make sure all eyes are on the story line and read the first time through together. When you have finished, go back to the start and let each child read a page until the book is finished again.

Reading Center:

Children will read today's book to their partner, then listen along while the other child reads. They should then spend time reading to each other books 1-8 as there is time. You will need three of each book for this center.

Initial Sound Hunt:

Use R100 and have the children write the sound each word starts with on the line under the pictures.

Journal:

Children will write and illustrate their work in their journals. If they want to write about Jig, that is great. One idea is to let them make up silly sentences using their new vocabulary: "The wig is in the rig." "The fig is in the pig." "Jig is in a wig." "Jig will dig in a wig."

ACROSS THE CURRICULUM

•Art - Have the children draw themselves in a funny outfit with a silly wig. They can share with the class what they are wearing and why they dressed up as they did.

•Science - Do a mini-unit on pigs learning why pigs stay in the mud in order to cool their bodies.

Here is a blurb on pigs from www.ag.ohio-state.edu

Why do pigs lie in mud?

Since March 1 is National Pig Day, Bob and I want to honor the snouted critter by busting the No. 1 myth of pigs: pigs aren't dirty animals.

Anyone who's been told to "Clean up that pigsty of a room!" knows that most people think the word pigsty is used to describe a dirty place. And, since pigsty is another word for pigpen, I guess it's easy to understand why you might think pigs are dirty animals.

Here's the truth: pigs prefer to keep themselves clean. The problem is that pigs can't sweat very much. Sweating helps you keep an even temperature. As sweat evaporates, it absorbs heat away from your body. Because hogs have very few sweat glands, they have to find other ways to keep cool. Pigs would much rather lounge in a clean pool of water, but that usually isn't an option. So, pigs lie in mud. The mud absorbs their bodies' excess heat. If pigs live inside barns, farmers make sure the temperature is just right for the future pork chops and bacon.

All in all, pigs get a bad rap about being messy. But once people learn the truth, they'll think pigs are full of smart stuff!

Scientifically yours,

Twig

---

46 Yy

OBJECTIVES
1. Child will gain a mental visual of Yy
2. Child will use this visual to recall Yy
3. Child will connect the visual to the sound
4. Child will utilize the visual in writing Yy
5. Child will blend using Yy

MATERIALS

1. *Alphabet Tales*, page 75
2. Alphabet Teaching Card for Yy
3. Yellow objects or book about yellow things
4. Pictures of items that start with Yy (R101)
5. Resources 101-103 (pp. 196-198)

ANTICIPATORY SET

Show the children your yellow objects or share the book about yellow things you found. Ask them to think of as many yellow things as they possibly can. Show the children the Alphabet Teaching Card for Yy and talk about why the girls might be yelling yippee yay! After the children have done some predictions, read the story.

STORY

Read the story for Yy and emphasize the sound for initial Y as you do. Let the children comment about the conglomeration the girls made to take to the fair. Would they have loved to have a bite?

VISUAL IMPRINTING

Ask the children to close their eyes and imagine seeing Yilly and Yolly yelling yippee yay. With their eyes still closed, ask the children to make the Yyy with their arms outraised like the girls did.

BODYSPELLING

uppercase & lowercase Y

Do the motion for Y together, using your right hands. Be sure and point out that both upper and lowercase Y are formed the same, and that the difference comes in the size and position of the letter on their writing paper.

WRITING

As you say the sound for Yy together aloud, the child(ren) will bodyspell, then practice forming the letter on their whiteboards. After the children have practiced writing Y, dictate these few words for them to sound and write on their whiteboards: YIP, YAP, YAM.
Brainstorm together other words that start with the

sound of Yy: YAK, YALE, YANKEE, YARD, YARN, YAWN, YEAR, YEAST, YESTERDAY, YOKE, YOOHOO, YORK, YOU, YOUNG, YOWL, YUCK, YUMMY.

BLENDING

Share R101. Show the children the letters for YIP, YAM, YAP. Say, "That's about all we have for now. Know why? It is because Y spends a lot of time acting other parts. He loves to pretend he's other people...like E and I (say long sounds of those letters). Let me show you what I mean." Use the words in R102 and teach the concept of final Y in one syllable words sounding like an I. Multi-syllable words ending with Y sound like an E on the end.

Line up the 1-syllable words in a column, then the 2-syllable words in another column. The words we are using in R102 are all words the children can decode once they understand the role of final Y. Draw attention to the three letter words (final I sound) first. Point to the starting sounds as being sounds they all know! Decode slowly each word. Have children clap for the number of syllables in each word (one).

Next, read the 2-syllable words, again, showing the initial sound, then clapping for the two syllables, emphasizing the E sound of the final Y.

CENTERS
Teacher Center:

Review journals with your group, making notes as they share of concepts they need to learn. Praise their writing.

Use the words you taught with final I and E sound for Y and ask the kids to show you two fingers for two syllable words and one finger for one syllable words.

Next, read the words again all mixed up and have the children give you a thumbs up when they hear a word that ends in the I sound.

Journal Center:

This group will update their journal to include their Yy words. Next they will choose a topic to write about, write at least one good sentence, then illustrate their writing.

Sorting Center:

Have children use the cut up words on R102, pasting them under the correct visual, E or I in R103.

Pocket Chart:

Use sight words in pocket chart to make sentences.

Scavenger Hunt:

Children will hunt for Y words in print -- both for initial Y and final Y. They could work with a partner and count how many words they find with initial Y and how many they find with final Y. They will need to identify the number of syllables in each word as well.

47 Nn

OBJECTIVES
1. Child will gain a mental visual of Nn
2. Child will use this visual to recall Nn
3. Child will connect the visual to the sound
4. Child will utilize the visual in writing Nn
5. Child will blend using Nn

MATERIALS

1. *Alphabet Tales*, page 79
2. Alphabet Teaching Card for Nn
3. Narrow and wide objects
4. Pictures of items that start with Nn (R104)
5. 6 copies of word family cards and letters for the blending work

ANTICIPATORY SET

Show the children your narrow and wide objects and then brainstorm together other objects that might fall into those categories. Ask "Which one is wide and which one is narrow:" Ocean/road, flagpole/parking lot, ruler/desktop, pencil/book, house/streetlight.

STORY

Read the story for Nn and emphasize the sound for N as you do. Let the children comment about the fact that Nelly and Ned sat behind each other all day and never noticed each other. Ask the children if they have ever been looking for something only to find out it was right under their nose.

VISUAL IMPRINTING

Ask the children to close their eyes and imagine seeing Ned and Nelly sitting on the ground. Were their backs next to each other, or away from each other? (next to). Which way were Ned's knees pointing? How about Nelly's knees?

BODYSPELLING

uppercase N   lowercase N

Do the motion for N together, using your left hand to make Ned's knees, with your right hand forming his back. Your right hand will make all of Nelly.

WRITING

As you say the sound of Nn together aloud, the child(ren) will bodyspell, then practice forming the letters on their whiteboards.
After the children have practiced writing N,

dictate these few words for them to sound and write on their whiteboards: NOT, NAP, NIP, NOD.
Now tell them the N sound will move to the end of the words: TAN, MAN, FAN, DAN, JAN, RAN, DIN, BIN, WIN.

BLENDING

Share R104. Put the word family endings in your pocket chart as before and use N for the rover. Your children should be able to blend pretty readily by this time, but go through the exercise to be sure. Let them tell you what each word will say. Use word families AT, OT, IT, AP, IP, OD, AG, AB, OB, IB, AN, to make NAT, NOT, NIT, NAP, NIP, NOD, NAG, NAB, NOB, NIB, NAN. Branch out into four sound words: SAND, LAND, BAND, POND, ANTS, PANT, PANTS, HINT, TINT, LINT.

CENTERS
Teacher Center:
Review journals with your group, making notes as they share of concepts they are missing. Praise their writing.
Review the final Y words from the previous lesson, sorting them and practicing clapping for number of syllables.
Use longer words for the children to clap syllables for, such as EMILY, NEWSPAPER, TELEVISION, SATELLITE, KITCHEN, LIVINGROOM, PLAYGROUND, PASSENGER, WATERMELON, ELEPHANT, HIPPOPOTAMUS.

Journal Center:
This group will update their journal to include their Nn words. Next they will choose a topic to write about, write at least one good sentence, then illustrate their writing.

Pocket Chart:
Use sight words in pocket chart to make sentences.

Scavenger Hunt:
Children will hunt for N words in print.

Sentence Unscramble:
You can make sentence strips out of the lines in the Easy-for-Me™ books. Put one sentence on each strip, cut apart into words, place each sentence in a zip lock baggie and use groups of six sentences in a center.

48 but, like, can  Uu

MATERIALS

1. SnapWords® List A, Group 3 displayed
2. Word family cards for UT and AN
3. A big umbrella
4. Alphabet Teaching Card for Uu
5. *Alphabet Tales*, page 83
6. Resource 105 (p. 200)

ANTicipatory SET

Show the children your umbrella and talk about when you got it; ask them how many of them have their very own umbrella. Talk about how most people use their umbrellas to keep the rain off them; some people in hot climates use their umbrellas to keep the hot sun off them so they won't get so sunburned. But in our story today, we are going to learn how one man used his umbrella for something totally different!

STORY/LESSON - BUT, LIKE, CAN
Read the story for Uu, emphasizing the short sound of Uu. The story is about Uncle Ule, and although his name contains both the long and short sounds of U, for today, focus on the short sound.

After the story, draw attention to the new sight words for today. Ask, "Do you see Uncle Ule's upside-down umbrella in one of these words?" When they have identified BUT as the one containing the umbrella, say, "So you know the sound that is in the middle of this word. What sound do we hear at the beginning? And at the end?" Blend B-U-T and do the language and motion on the reverse side of the card.

Next, sound CAN together and repeat the teaching steps as for BUT.

Teach LIKE in the same way. Use in the sentence, and in others: "Mike will like my bike." Let the children take turns telling you something they like.

WRITING

Start with the word BUT. Do Quick Draw with the word, sounding and writing as per the directions. Next use that same word family and have them write HUT, NUT, CUT, GUT, JUT, RUT. When you have checked boards, start with the word family AN. Play Quick Draw using these words: CAN, FAN, TAN, PAN, DAN, BAN, JAN, RAN, NAN. Check boards.

Dictate: "Dan is tan." "Jan ran to Nan." "Dan ran, but not Jan."

CENTERS
Teacher Center:

Focus on LIKE in your center. Tell the children that they are going to help you do a little skit about someone named Pinchy E. Write the letters for LIKE, one letter per notecard. Give a letter each to four children, lining them up in order to spell LIKE. Tell them that E doesn't really say anything at all because he's so busy being sneaky. While the other guys are saying a sound, he's busy reaching behind K and pinching Ii. When he pinches Ii, Ii gets startled and says his name "I" (long sound, not short sound). Guide the children into sounding out the word. The child holding L will say Ll when you point to her, the child holding Ii will say long Ii louder because Sneaky E is pinching him at that moment. K then says Kkk (sound of letter). Blend together to say LIKE. You may repeat this little play with four different children using other words such as MIKE, BIKE, HIKE, DIKE. Switch vowels and do the same play with AKE words: LAKE, CAKE, TAKE, BAKE, WAKE. Let the children end the lesson by looking though books to find words with the Pinchy E in them.

Pocket Chart Center:
Making sentences with sight words to write in center folders. Use the word HAS along with their current sight words and the name cards of class members. You also could make available color words on cards.

Scavenger Hunt:
Children will look for their new sight words in print.

Journal:
Children will write in their journals. Today it would be good to encourage them to make sentences using LIKE..."I like cats, but I do not like dogs." "I can sit, but I do not like to." Also they will add their new sound and word families.

Children might want to write about an unusual use for a large umbrella and then illustrate their writing.

Assessments:
Continue to keep up on the Skills Tracking form.

MORE
Explore with the children the origins of umbrellas. You might start by going to this website:

http://inventors.about.com/library/inventors/blumbrella.htm

OBJECTIVES
1. Child will successfully read *My Dog, Jip*
2. Child will write the story line from dictation
3. Child will correctly sequence events in the story

MATERIALS

1. *My Dog, Jip*, six copies
2. Sentence strips for the book text
3. Resource 106 (p. 102)
4. "Stocked" centers
5. A book about a pet puppy

ANTICIPATORY SET

Share your book with the children in preparation for our story today. When you have finished, ask the children how many of them have a pet dog at home. Let them talk about that for a few minutes, and lead the discussion into how their dog behaves in the house. Tell the children you have a story to read today about a pet dog named Jip who got into some trouble in the house.

LESSON

Before you read the sentence strips, introduce the new vocabulary that will appear in this book: NIP (little bites), YIP (short incessant barks), SIP (a little drink), TIP (to push something over), RIP (to tear). Look for all the words that have IP at the end. Read the strips to the children first, then have them read with you as you listen for all voices and make sure all children are participating.

WRITING

Play Quick Draw with the children using their new IP family. Use the words in the book first: JIP, NIP, RIP, SIP, TIP, YIP. Continue with review of some U words: HUT, GUT, BUT, JUT, NUT, RUT. Then HUM, GUM, BUM, YUM, RUM. Then DUD, BUD. DUG, HUG, LUG, BUG, JUG, RUG. DUN, GUN, BUN, NUN, RUN. Finish with RUB, NUB.

Before breaking into groups, review some Pinchy E words: CUBE, LUBE, TUBE, LAKE, SAKE, CAKE, CONE, BONE, LONE, PETE, LIKE, MIKE, BIKE.

CENTERS
Teacher Center:

Review student journals before reading the book for today, making notes of teaching points from the students' writing.

Give each child at the table a copy of the book *My Dog, Jip.* Read the cover, then title page, then move to page two. Make sure all eyes are on the story line, and read the first time through together. When you have finished, go back to the start and let each child read a page until the book is finished again.

During the reading of the book, focus on using pictures and illustrations as cues for reading. Model this practice for your children and praise them when you see that they are using pictures to cue their reading. Do one

last quick review of the meaning of the IP words in the book if you feel it is necessary.

Reading Center:

Children will read today's book to their partner, then listen along while the other child reads. They should then spend time reading to each other their previous books as there is time.

Picture/Word Match:

Use R106, and have the children write the sounds each word starts with on the line under the pictures.

If the picture is a word they know or can decode, they should write the whole word.

Journal:

Children will write and illustrate their work in their journals. If they want to write about their dog or Jip, great.

MORE

Make a class book about the children's pets, real or imaginary. Each student will make a page showing a picture or drawing of their pet, them taking care of the pet, and doing their favorite thing with their pet.

Want to explore more? Check out http://www. wikihow.com/Care-for-Puppies.

OBJECTIVES
1. Child will successfully read *I Can Hop*
2. Child will write the story line from dictation
3. Child will correctly sequence events in the story
4. Child will learn sight word STOP

MATERIALS

1. *I Can Hop*, six copies
2. Sentence strips for the book text
3. Resources 107-108 (pp. 202-203)
4. SnapWords® Card for STOP

ANTICIPATORY SET

Share Resources information (R107) about hogs and bogs. The children will understand that the hog in this story is not a cute little pink piglet with a curly tail! Ask the children how many of them have heard of a pogo stick? Seen one? Been on one? Do they think they would like to have a pogo stick and be able to hop around in big bounds? Tell the children that the boy in this story had a pogo stick and it ended up getting him in a little bit of trouble!

LESSON - Sight Word STOP

Point out the sight word STOP, drawing attention to the fact that all the sounds are very familiar to them! They can easily sound out the word. Ask the children to be alert as you read today's book to see who can find the word STOP in the story.

The word families to draw attention to in this book are the OP and OG word families. Analyze the story line before you read it together, identifying the sight words in the story, as well as words that repeat. Then read the sentence strips together with everyone participating. One way to make sure all children are right there reading and thinking is to divide the class into two groups and have the groups take turns reading as you point to them. If they don't know when they will be called on to read, they will need to follow along and be ready. Those that are not "on" should whisper read along with the group that is reading.

WRITING

Play Quick Draw with the children using their OP and OG words. Words to use include: HOP, LOP, BOP, COP, MOP, TOP, POP, STOP. DOG, HOG, LOG, BOG, JOG, FROG (Be sure to sound each sound separately: F-R-O-G, as blends are made of two distinct sounds).

Dictate: "I can hop on a mop." "I can not hop on pop!" "I do not hop on the hog!" "I can not hop. Now I will stop."

CENTERS
Teacher Center:

Review student journals before reading the book for today, making notes of teaching points from the students' writing.

Give each child at the table a copy of the book *I Can Hop*. Read the cover, title page, then move to page two. Make sure all eyes are on the story line and read the first time through together. When you have finished, go back to the start and let each child read a page until the book is finished again.

Again the focus during the reading of the book today is on using pictures and illustrations as cues for reading. Model this practice for your children and praise them when you see that they are using pictures to cue their reading.

Test comprehension of the story line by asking the children to tell you without referring to the book, which are the things that the boy said he could hop on. Then ask which things he could not hop on. Then ask, "Why did the boy say he could not hop on the hog or the dog?" Their answers should reflect their understanding that the animals might get cranky with the boy.

Reading Center:
Children will read today's book to their partner, then listen along while the other child reads. They should then spend time reading to each other their previous books as there is time.

Picture/Sentence Match:
Use R108 and have the children cut out the sentences provided and glue each one under the picture that best illustrates the meaning of each sentence.

Journal:
Children will write and illustrate their work in their journals. They might want to write about themselves and their pogo stick (real or imagined) and where THEY would hop.

ACROSS THE CURRICULUM
• Social Studies - Study transportation. What are recommended ways to get places? What if you have to cross an ocean? Go around the block? Go into the city? Go to another state?

• Art - Have the children invent their own means of transportation as a spin-off of the pogo stick. They should draw their concept and share it with the class, explaining how their creation is more useful or fun than what is currently available to us!

51 get, play, down*

MATERIALS

1. SnapWords® List A Group 3 displayed
2. Resource 109 & center materials
3. SnapWords® List A, Group 4
4. Letter cards for N, D, F, R, C, L, B, S, P
5. OW, ET, AND, and AY on plain cards
6. Stocked centers

ANTICIPATORY SET

Gather the children around you and the List A Group 3 SnapWords® in the pocket chart. Review the known words as needed, playing Activity 9 in Appendix A.

LESSON - Sight Words DOWN, PLAY, GET

Introduce the new sight words for today as you always do, talking about the picture, and using the motions and language on the reverse. Then arrange them in your pocket chart like this: "Get down and play." Ask the children to imagine where the child is that is spoken to in this sentence. Could he be up in a treehouse or a slide? Let them make up a place for the child to get down from, then ask who is inviting him down and why.

Remind the children of the OW sound spelling in the center of DOWN. Remind them it is the same sound spelling as they had in the sight word NOW.

Place the card with OW written on it in the pocket chart. Next place the letter cards in a column on the left of the OW card, and the N card at the end of OW. You want it to be OWN as in DOWN. Tell the children you are going to investigate which available letters can go on the front of OWN to make words. Of course, the D will make their new word for today. Next, make CLOWN, BROWN, FROWN, TOWN, sounding out each word. You will sound like this: C-L-OW-N, B-R-OW-N, F-R-OW-N, T-OW-N.

Say, "The brown clown will frown downtown."

Next, display the AY card in your pocket chart and repeat, teaching the children that these two letters make ONE sound together. Make these words: NAY, DAY, RAY, LAY, BAY, SAY, PAY. Also, STAY, SPAY, GRAY, TRAY, SPRAY.

Next display ET and make: NET, LET, BET, SET, PET.

WRITING

Because today is the end of List A, Group 3, practice finding and writing the plain words using the reverse side of the stylized cards. You will say, "Find and write GET." Children will write on their whiteboards. Continue like this, doing quick visual checks, until all the Group 3 words have been located and written.
Play Activity 5 - Around the World.

GRADUATION!

Tell the children that today is the day you will "graduate" Group 3 words to the classroom word wall. Make a big deal out of posting the plain green word wall words to the wall while the children are watching. Next, take out List A, Group 4 words and place them one at a time in the pocket chart as you briefly introduce each word as you have done each time.

CENTERS
Teacher Center:

Review children's journals. Introduce the concept of compound words: INTO, ONTO, TODAY, TREEHOUSE, PLAYHOUSE, NOBODY.

The children can play Go Fish or "War" in 3's from Activity 5. While the children are doing this, take time to pull one child aside at a time and do formal assessments on their sight words.

Pocket Chart Center:

Making sentences with sight words to write in center folders. Include their new words.

Scavenger Hunt:

Children will look for their new sight words in print, cut them out and glue on paper, or highlight them with a yellow crayon.

Sentence Unscramble:

Use R109.

52 we, said, little, come

© 2007 Sarah Major

OBJECTIVES
1. Child will review word wall words and new words
2. Child will learn sight words WE, SAID, LITTLE, COME
3. Child will revisit compound words
4. Child will use sight words in sentences
5. Child will learn five nouns

MATERIALS

1. SnapWords® List A, Group 4 displayed
2. R110 (see binder pocket) & R111
3. Letter cards for M, H, S, T
4. Magazines or newspapers
5. A big book with lots of SAIDs in it
6. Plain words on cards for THE, TO, CAT
7. Red and Blue words on cards (see teacher center)

ANTicipatory SET

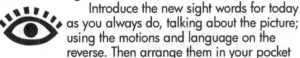

Gather the children around you and the List A Group 4 SnapWords® in the pocket chart. Review the sight words for the purpose of the children being able to correctly call the words while seeing the stylized side. Play Activities 2, 3, 4, 5 as desired.

LESSON - Sight Words WE, SAID, LITTLE, COME

Introduce the new sight words for today as you always do, talking about the picture; using the motions and language on the reverse. Then arrange them in your pocket chart like this: "We said come to the little cat." Use the SnapWords® for the new words in this sentence.

Share with the children that when we say "sight words," we generally are talking about words that are hard to sound out, and words that we use all the time when we read. Three of today's words are truly sight words: they are very hard to sound out. In fact, SAID cannot be sounded out because the sound picture AI usually says long A sound, but in this word it just sounds like the short sound for E (EH as in EGG).

Draw attention to the word SAID and then find the word in a big book in which dialog forms a great part of the story. Explain that we use this word all the time when we talk, and if we read what people are saying, we will see this word very often. As you read the big book, have the children do the silent thumbs up every time you come to a SAID.

Display LITTLE. Point out the double TT in the middle and remind the children that when there are two letters the same, they are just helping each other say ONE sound, not two. Next point out the LE at the end of the word. Share that there are many words in English that end with LE and you just say the sound for L. Share next that one way to remember how to write LITTLE is to say it funny. Say it like this "LITT-LEE." For a visual help, let the children underline TT and circle LE on their whiteboards.

Finally show display COME and share once again

that they cannot decode this word. Ask what would happen to COME if you took the C off the front and used an S instead? SOME would be the new word. You can use these two words to say, "Some cats can come."

WE is an easy word to learn, and you can do sound replacement for the W to make rhyming words: HE, SHE, BE, ME, SEE.

WRITING

Play "Find and Write" with the children using the sight words in your pocket chart. You will call out a word, and they will find it in the pocket chart and write it on their whiteboards. You will do a quick visual check as you go.

Then dictate, "Come little cat." "I said come to the cat." "Come and play." "We can come and play." "A little cat sat."

CENTERS
Teacher Center:

Review children's journals as usual. Using R110, introduce the new words that will appear in Lesson 53's book, *Do Stop*. The words are: HOUSE, BALL, GRASS, TREE, SAND. Ask the children to make up sentences using the new words, and while they do, continue individual assessment on List A, Group 3 words if needed.

Review compound words. Write in blue on small cards: sand, tree, base, sun, snow, in, day, play. Write in red: box, house, ball, shine, ball, side, time, time. Have the children make compound words using a blue word and a red word. All words will be used up to make: sandbox, treehouse, baseball, sunshine, snowball, inside, daytime, playtime. Leave the new noun words displayed for reference as the children work on this activity.

Pocket Chart Center:

Making sentences with sight words from Group 4 to write in center folders. Incorporate the new noun words.

Scavenger Hunt:

Children will look for their new sight words in print, cut them out and glue on paper, or highlight them with a yellow crayon. Challenge them to find and cut out words with which to make whole sentences (somewhat like ransome notes in movies!).

Sentence Unscramble:

Same procedure as before. Use R111.

53 📖 Book 12 - Do Stop

MATERIALS

1. *Do Stop*, six copies
2. Sentence strips for the book text
3. R110 and R112 (p. 106)

ANTICIPATORY SET

Ask the children to share with the class their favorite things to do when they have friends over. Do they prefer to play outside? Inside? Active games, or quiet games? Let all the children share who want to, and then tell them that in your new book, a little boy called his friend on the phone to invite her over to play. He was telling his friend all the fun things they could do if she came over. Let the children predict what the children might play together.

LESSON

The primary focus in this book is not word families. It is, rather, the new nouns, and the sight words, along with color words. Analyze the text you have posted on sentence strips, looking for WE, CAN, PLAY, STOP. Next, find the five nouns in the strips. Share with the children that once again, they are going to need their skill of using pictures as cues for decoding. If they see a ball in the picture, for instance, they are likely to have no trouble reading the word BALL on that page.

Read the sentence strips together in chorus. Pay attention to trouble spots.

WRITING

Dictate short sentences from the book for the children to write. Start with "Do stop by my house." Show the children that in HOUSE, there are only three sounds because two of the sounds have two letters: H-OU-SE. Share that other words match this word and practice writing on whiteboards: MOUSE, LOUSE, DOUSE. Share that many words in English end in SE just like they learned about LE. The two letters together just say L or S. They should be on the lookout for these letter combinations in books.*

Dictate, "We can go and not stop." "We can get a ball." "We will play." "We will run." "We will go up." "We will go down."

Other spellings that follow this pattern: se-house, ve-live, ze-sneeze, ge-cage, ce-ice, re-were, le-simple. I would initiate a search to span several days in which children collect words that match each of these words. Hang vertical strips of paper to a bulletin board, one per spelling and write or glue the words the children find under each sample word given.

CENTERS

Teacher Center:

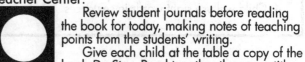

Review student journals before reading the book for today, making notes of teaching points from the students' writing.

Give each child at the table a copy of the book *Do Stop*. Read together the cover, title page, and then move to page two. Make sure all eyes are on the story line and read the first time through together. When you have finished, go back to the start and let each child read a page until the book is finished again.

Again the focus during the reading of the book today is on using pictures and illustrations as cues for reading. Model this practice for your children and praise them when you see that they are using pictures to cue their reading.

Check for comprehension of the story by asking: "What colors are the ball in the story?" (red and yellow). "When they were playing 'down,' what were they playing with?" (sand in sand box). "When they were playing up, where were they?" (the big tree). "When the children played in the green grass, what were they playing with?" (the red and yellow ball).

Reading Center:
Children will read today's book to their partner, then listen along while the other child reads. They should then spend time reading to each other their previous books as there is time.

Picture/Sentence Match:
Use R112 and have the children cut out the sentences provided and glue them under the picture that best illustrates the meaning of each sentence.

Journal:
Children will write and illustrate their work in their journals. They might want to write about playing with a friend who comes over to their house.

54 want, did, you, here

OBJECTIVES
1. Child will review word wall words & new words
2. Child will learn sight words WANT, DID, YOU, HERE
3. Child will find these words in print
4. Child will use sight words in sentences

MATERIALS

1. SnapWords® List A, Group 4 displayed
2. R110, R113-114 (pp. 207-209)
3. Letter cards for Y, S, G, R, P
4. Magazines or newspapers
5. ERE, OU, TH, WH on cards

ANTICIPATORY SET

Gather the children around you and the List A Group 4 SnapWords® in the pocket chart. Review the sight words for the purpose of the children being able to correctly call the words while seeing the stylized side. Play Activities 2, 3, 4, 5 as desired.

LESSON - Sight Words WANT, DID, YOU, HERE

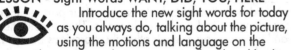

Introduce the new sight words for today as you always do, talking about the picture, using the motions and language on the reverse. Then arrange them in your pocket chart like this: "Did you want it here?" Use the SnapWords® for the new words in this sentence.

Start with DID, as it is the simplest. Play a sound replacement game to make these words: HID, BID, SID, MID, SLID. Teach the children that when we use DID to ask a question, it will be the first word we say. EX: "Did you clean your room?"

Next, display YOU and teach that the word has only two sounds: Y-OO. Use the Y and OU cards to make YOU, and then make S-OU-P, G-R-OU-P using the individual letters. Then write, "You eat soup in a group," writing the OU in each of the three words in a different color so the sound spelling stands out vividly.

Display WANT. Tell the children that they cannot really sound out WANT because the A is acting a bit funny in this word. Maybe it is showing off and trying to sound fancy, because instead of the Aaa sound in ANT, it is saying the AH sound you make when the doctor tells you to open wide! Write, "I want water, father." and write the A in the words in a different color. Tell the children that in these three words, the A sounds all fancy and says AH. Next, write "I want an ant." Write all three ANs in a contrasting color, and point out that the word WANT has the word ANT in it. This might help them remember the word when they come across it in their reading. Use R114 as you teach WANT.

Finally display ERE card and SnapWords® HERE. Tell the children that when they are reading about where

something is, the words they will see will have the ERE on the end. Tell them the R is the baloney in the sandwich, while the E's are the bread. Show them what happens to ERE when you put WH on the front. It becomes WHERE If you place the TH on the front, the word changes to THERE. Use the three words in a little story, changing the beginning spellings as you go. Say, "Pretend you are hungry and Mom makes you a sandwich. You are playing and she calls to you. 'Martin, come HERE! I have a sandwich for you!' You come in the kitchen and you say, 'WHERE is my sandwich?' and Mom points her finger and says 'THERE is your baloney sandwich.'" Use R113 to reinforce this concept.

WRITING

Practice writing the mini-lessons you just gave your children. For instance, have them write HERE. Then prompt them to change the word to THERE (the T looks like an arm pointing THERE). Then have them change the word to WHERE. (The W looks like someone's elbows pointing down as they gesture the question WHERE?) Dictate, "I am here." "The cat is here." "My mom is here." Write, "Did you come here?" "Did you want it?" Have the children glance at the sight words if needed before they write, but try and discourage their copying letter for letter. They need to utilize other ways to remember such as visualization.

CENTERS
Teacher Center:

Review children's journals as usual. Using R110, introduce/review the new words that will appear in lesson 53's book, *Little Dab*. The words are: SUN, CRAB, and SAND. Ask the children to make up sentences using the new words, and while they do, continue individual assessment on List A, Group 3 words if needed.

Pocket Chart Center:

Making sentences with sight words from Group 4 to write in center folders. Alternately, the children can make a short sentence, put it in a snack baggie, and exchange with a partner. When they have unscrambled their sentences, they will write them in their center folders.

Scavenger Hunt:

Children will look for their new sight words in print, cut them out and glue on paper, or highlight them with a yellow crayon.

Sentence Unscramble:

Same procedure as before. Use previous resources.

OBJECTIVES
1. Child will successfully read *Little Dab*
2. Child will write the story line from dictation
3. Child will correctly sequence events in the story
4. Child will review SAND, and will learn SUN, CRAB

MATERIALS

1. *Little Dab*, six copies
2. Sentence strips for the book text
3. Big book about crabs, or story book
4. R110, R115-R117 (pp. 211-213)

ANTICIPATORY SET

Ask the children what they know about crabs. Record their contributions on your whiteboard or easel pad. Next, introduce your information on crabs, or share your story with the children. Discuss other beach creatures such as seagulls, pelicans, jellyfish, etc. Tell the children that today you will have a story about a crab who just loved being by the ocean playing in the sand and the waves.

LESSON

Share your words from Resource 110: SUN and CRAB. The children will be able to decode CRAB. Brainstorm rhyming words for CRAB such as GAB, LAB, JAB, NAB, DAB, GRAB, TAB then draw attention to the story on sentence strips. There are a few words in the AB family, but our primary focus is on recognizing the sight words the children have learned from List A Group 4 so far: WANT, COME, HERE, SAID, DID, HERE, LITTLE, YOU. They will have the word CRAB and DIG to decode as well as the names of the other two crabs: RAB and GAB.

Introduce with this book, the use of quotation marks as marks that bracket what someone is saying. Some children have a lot of trouble understanding where to place quotation marks, so they will need plenty of practice identifying the words someone actually said.

Write these short sentences on your whiteboard:
Mom said, "Come here!"
I said, "Can I play?"
My cat said, "MEOW!"

Walk the children through identifying which words were actually spoken, and circle them.

Read the sentence strips as usual. The second time through, choose three children to be Little Dab, Gab, and Rab, and act out the story with the children saying only the lines spoken by those characters. You would read, "Rab said," and the child who is Rab would say "Do you want to come up here?"

WRITING:

Play Quick Draw with the AB words. Then dictate "Little Dab is a crab." "Big Rab is a crab." "Gab will play down here." "I can play here." "Dab can not come up."

CENTERS
Teacher Center:

Review student journals before reading the book for today, making notes of teaching points from the students' writing.

Give each child at the table a copy of the book *Little Dab*. Read together the cover, title page, and then move to page two. Make sure all eyes are on the story line and read the first time through together. When you have finished, go back to the start and let each child read a page until the book is finished again.

Use Resource 115 for practice with the children in identifying the words that are spoken. The children will read the sentences with you and then will color the spoken words yellow. Teach them that the word SAID and its comma are clues that someone is about to say something. After the children have colored the spoken words yellow, teach them how to make quotation marks - before and after the yellow spoken words. Depending on how the children did with you in the center, you might want to re-copy this page and have them repeat the activity for homework or in a center.

Reading Center:
Children will read today's book to their partner, then listen along while the other child reads. They should then spend time reading to each other their previous books as there is time.

Sight Word Search:
Using R116, the children will practice finding and coloring their sight words from List A Group 4. Extra words that appear within the large words are listed in the directions.

Journal:
Children will write and illustrate their work in their journals. They might want to write about playing with a friend who comes over to their house.

ACROSS THE CURRICULUM
• Science - Study crabs and other shore/beach/ocean creatures.
• Geography - Using the world map, help the children identify where the oceans are and color the water in them blue. Introduce the Atlantic Ocean and the Pacific Ocean. Next, find the other oceans in our world and color them blue as well. (R117)

56 look, for

OBJECTIVES
1. Child will review word wall words & new words
2. Child will learn sight words LOOK, FOR
3. Child will learn two sounds for OO
4. Child will find these words in print
5. Child will use sight words in sentences

MATERIALS

1. SnapWords® List A Group 4 displayed
2. Resource 118-120 (pp. 214-216)
3. Letter cards for L, B, C, T, N, B, R, C
4. Magazines or newspapers
5. OOK on a plain card
6. Stocked centers

ANTICIPATORY SET

Gather the children around you and the List A Group 4 SnapWords® in the pocket chart. Review the sight words to determine if the children can correctly call the words while seeing the stylized side. Play Activities 2, 3, 4, 5 as desired from page 282.

LESSON - Sight Words LOOK, FOR

Introduce the new sight words for today as usual: talking about the picture and using the motions and language on the reverse.

Then arrange them in your pocket chart like this: "I will LOOK FOR you." Use SnapWords® for the new words in this sentence.

Place the OOK card in your pocket chart, and place all the single letters to the left in a column. Teach the children that in this sight word, OOK can be a family. Sound it together: OO-K. Next make new words by adding the letters to the front of OOK: LOOK, BOOK, COOK, TOOK, NOOK, BROOK, CROOK. Say, "The cook took a look at the book in a nook by the brook."

Next, introduce FOR. Draw attention to the OR in the word, tying it to the word they learned several lessons back. Tell the children that OR is a very common letter sequence and that sometimes we find it in the beginning of a word, sometimes in the middle, and sometimes on the end. Write on your whiteboard or display cards with these words on them: PORCH, PORTER, ORDER, TORCH, FORTY, CANDOR, FAVOR, BEFORE, ADORE, ORGAN, ORBIT, ORCA, ORAL. Write the ORs in a contrasting color within each word. The children will be able to decode some of the words, but the main point is to show the various positions of the sound spelling OR, and to accustom the children to reading the letters as a small embedded word, rather than decoding them one sound at a time.

WRITING
Play Quick Draw with the OOK words. You could add the AB words, or any other word family you would like to review. Then, dictate: "I will look for you." "He will look for it." "We can look for you." "Will you look for me?"

CENTERS
Teacher Center:
Review children's journals as usual.

Teach two sound spellings for OO using R119-120. Supervise the children as they sort the words on R119.

Use the following words to practice sound discrimination. The children will listen for the vowel sound and will bodyspell the vowel they hear in each word: Aa, Oo, Uu, or Ii. Use these words: BAT, FIT, MITT, CUP, MOP, SIT, UP, ON, IT, SNAP, STOP, FLIP, FLOP, FLUB, SLUB, SNIP, CLAP, TRIP, FLOG, SLIP.

Next, you will say the sounds of the words in the chart below, and the children will identify the words you are segmenting. Leave a half second between the sounds so that each sound is clearly heard.

4-SOUNDS	5 SOUNDS	6-PLUS
F-L-A-P	S-T-U-M-P	S-T-R-A-N-G-ER
C-L-I-P	F-L-O-P-S	P-A-N-C-A-KE
S-I-LL-Y	P-L-A-N-T	S-P-I-N-A-CH
H-A-PP-Y	S-T-A-N-D	F-L-A-G-P-O-LE
T-E-N-T	F-L-A-G-S	P-L-AY-M-A-TE
S-A-N-D	S-P-I-N-Y	D-O-L-PH-I-N
P-O-S-T	S-K-U-N-K	S-E-P-T-E-M-B-ER

Pocket Chart Center:
Making sentences with sight words from Group 4 to write in center folders. Include new words and some OO words as well.

Scavenger Hunt:
Children will look for their new sight words in print, cut them out and glue on paper, or highlight them with a yellow crayon. They should also look for words that have the sound spellings OO and OO as learned today.

Making Sight Words:
Put the letters that make sight words into baggies. Give each child a copy of R118 and tell them the words they will be making are found in the word bank. If you would prefer, they may refer to your pocket chart with List A Group 4 words in it. There are enough words for the whole group.

Journal:
The children should continue to journal daily. Encourage them to use their new sight words in their writing.

57 call, this*

MATERIALS

1. SnapWords® List A Group 4 displayed
2. Resources 121-122 (pp. 217-218)
3. Letter cards for M, T, F, B, H, W
4. SnapWords® List A Group 5
5. ALL, IS, HIS on plain cards
6. Nouns recently learned on plain cards

ANTICIPATORY SET

Review the SnapWords® from List A Group 4 that you have displayed in your pocket chart. Today is the day to graduate this group of words to the classroom word wall. Tell the children that before you move the words, they will need to say goodbye to them. They will turn over the words one at a time, starting with the words they feel are the very easiest to remember. Have the children vote the words off as described in Activity 9, Word Flip.

When all the words have been turned over, post them to the classroom wall and then place the List A Group 5 words in the pocket chart. Do Activity 1 with these words.

LESSON - Sight Words CALL, THIS

Introduce the new sight words for today as you always do, talking about the picture, using the motions and language on the reverse. Then arrange them in your pocket chart like this: "I can CALL THIS dog." Use the stylized word cards for the new words in this sentence.

Place the ALL card in your pocket chart, and place all the single letters to the left in a column. Teach the children that in the sight word CALL, ALL can be a word family. Say together: ALL. Next make new words by adding the letters to the front of ALL: MALL, TALL, FALL, BALL, HALL, WALL. Say, "The ball will fall from the tall wall in the hall of the mall."

Next, introduce THIS. Ask the children if they can find two little words inside THIS. (Show IS, HIS). Of course the S in THIS is a soft Spotty Snake sound, while IS and HIS have the fizzing Z sound. Cover the IS in THIS and point out that THIS starts out just like THE. Emphasize the TH sound in both words as you say them. Sentence to write for this: "This is his." The word THIS is a magic word with a whole sentence inside of it.

WRITING

Play Quick Draw with the ALL words. Have the children invent sentences using the ALL words and choose a short one to dictate to the children. Ideas: "The hall in the mall is tall." "The ball is in the hall of the mall." "The mall is tall." "The ball will fall."

Next focus on THIS. Dictate the sentence, "This is his." Then add other sentences such as "This is his cap." "This cap is his." "The red cap is his."

Be sure the children update their journals regularly with new sight words and word families.

CENTERS
Teacher Center:

Review children's journals as usual. Use R122 to guide a comprehension activity for Little Dab. The children will cut out the pictures provided and place them in the correct order as they occurred in the story.

Then, ask the children why they think Little Dab didn't play with Gab or Rab.

Finally, lead an auditory discrimination activity. The words you use will be from the ALL and ILL families. The children are to bodyspell either Ii or Aa depending on the vowel that appears in each word you say. Use these words: Fall, fill, wall, will, still, stall, mill, mall, till, tall, small, call.

Pocket Chart Center:

Making sentences with sight words from Group 4 to write in center folders. In addition to the current sight words, give the children the nouns they have recently learned to use with their sight words, as well as the OO words from Lesson 56.

Scavenger Hunt:

Children will look for their new sight words in print, cut them out and glue on paper, or highlight them with a yellow crayon.

Making Words:

Use R121. This time, instead of using cut-up letters to make words, the children will use the letters provided to make words to match the pictures. For example, for the picture of BALL, they will glue the B from the letter bank by an ALL to label the picture.

Journal:

Continue daily journaling.

58 📖 Book 14 - Bob Hums

OBJECTIVES
1. Child will successfully read *Bob Hums*
2. Child will write the story line from dictation
3. Child will correctly sequence events in the story
4. Child will review use of quotation marks
5. Child will learn to add S for plurals and actions

MATERIALS

1. *Bob Hums*, six copies
2. Sentence strips for the book text
3. Harmonica
4. Resources 115, 123-124 (pp. 219-220)

ANTICIPATORY SET

Share with the children your harmonica and blow some notes so they can hear the distinctive sound of the music. Show the children that even if your mouth stays in the same place, the sound changes depending on whether you are blowing out or sucking air in. Ask them if they have ever played a harmonica.

LESSON

The primary word family in *Bob Hums* is the UM family. Orally, generate other UM words with the children. (HUM, BUM, RUM, SUM, YUM, GUM, STRUM, SLUM).

Review the use of quotation marks with your children. You might want to re-teach, using R115. Tell the children that they will be seeing quotation marks in this story.

Do a search for words that repeat, quotation marks, and sight words they have just learned. Now read the story line together.

After you have read the story line, ask the children to imagine why the big man told Bob and the child that they could not stay where they were and make music. There is no right answer, but possible reasons could be that they were sitting on a bench that belonged to someone else, or that they had been there for a while and the patrol wanted them to move on. Ask the children where they think Bob and the child walked to in order to find their big tree to sit under.

WRITING

Play Quick Draw with the UM words, then dictate short sentences: "Look for this." "Call for this." "This is for me." "Look at me." "You can call now." "This is big." "This will look big." "This is not little."

Here are some additional words that have U as a vowel: CUP, CUT, HUT, LUG, BUG, SNUG, DUD, BUD, CUD, MUD, RUB, TUB, CUB, SUB, DUN, GUN, BUN, RUN, FUN, SUN.

Finally, play an auditory-to-visual game. Say "Write CUP. Now, change the U to an A in your imagination and say the new word. CAP. Now write CAP." In like manner do the following: DUD to DID. LUG to LAG. BUG to BIG to BAG. HUT to HIT to HOT to HAT. MUD to MAD. RUB to RIB to ROB. BUD to BAD to BID to BOD.

CENTERS
Teacher Center:

Review student journals before reading the book for today, making notes of teaching points from the students' writing.

Give each child at the table a copy of the book *Bob Hums*. Read together the cover, title page, then move to page two. Make sure all eyes are on the story line and read the first time through together. When you have finished, go back to the start and let each child read a page until the book is finished again.

Teach the concept of adding an S to a word such as in changing LIKE to LIKES. HIT to HITS, RUN to RUNS, HUM to HUMS. Tell the children that if we are talking about what we or another person is doing, we add an S. If we say "Bob can hum" it just means that Bob knows how to hum. If we say "Bob hums," we are talking about something he does. Examples include: "Bob likes apples." "Bob runs on the sidewalk." "Bob makes dinner." "Bob walks his dog." All these are things Bob does as part of his life. Have the children come up with examples talking about someone in their family or their pet. Ex: "Fido barks at night."

Teach also the concept of more than one, and how when we are talking about more than one, we add an S at the end of the word. Have the children use their whiteboards as you say a word for them to write. Next prompt them to change the word to make it mean "more than one." Words to use: CAP, CAT, HAT, BAT, COT, TOP, TIP, BALL, HALL, GILL, HILL, GUM, BUD, SUN.

Reading Center:
Children will read today's book to their partner, then listen along while the other child reads.

Plurals:
Using R124, the children will practice plurals by writing the word under each picture that best describes it. For ex: if there is one bat in the picture, they will write BAT. If the picture shows more than one bat, they will write BATS.

Journal:
Children will write and illustrate their work in their journals.

Pocket Chart:
Making sentences with sight words. Supply blank cards for children to use in writing nouns with plurals on them, such as CATS, CAPS, etc. Model one sentence for them in the top row, then they can create their own below yours. Idea for your sentence: "I see two cats." Or "My cats like to play here."

Story Sequence:
Use R123.

59 have, make, ran

OBJECTIVES
1. Child will begin List A, Group 5 SnapWords®
2. Child will learn sight words HAVE, MAKE, RAN
3. Child will find these words in print
4. Child will use sight words in sentences
5. Child will learn the use of past tense
6. Child will review "Pinchy E"

MATERIALS

1. SnapWords® List A Group 5 displayed
2. Resource 125 (p. 221)
3. Letter cards for D, B, J, R, M, C, T
4. Magazines or newspapers
5. AKE, AN on plain cards

ANTicipatory SET

Review the SnapWords® from List A Group 5 that you have displayed in your pocket chart. Review the ALL words you taught in the previous sight word lesson. One option is to say ALL. Then hold up the letter M and ask the children what word M+ALL would make. MALL. Next hold up a B and ask for the new word (BALL), then a T (TALL), an H (HALL), an F (FALL).

LESSON - Sight Words HAVE, MAKE, RAN

Introduce the new sight words for today as you always do, talking about the picture; using the motions and language on the reverse. Then arrange them in your pocket chart like this: "I HAVE to MAKE my bed." "I RAN out." Use the SnapWords® for the new words in this sentence.

Place the AKE card in your pocket chart, and place all the single letters to the left in a column. Replay the "Pinchy E" skit, using four volunteers if you feel the children need a reminder of the role of Pinchy E in the word MAKE. Then ask the children to tell you each new word you can make as you place the intial letter sound in front of the AKE card: BAKE, JAKE, RAKE, CAKE, TAKE, LAKE. Silly sentence for AKE: "Jake will bake a cake to take to the lake."

Next, introduce HAVE. Ask the children if they think Pinchy E is in this word. Doubtless the children will see the E and assume it will follow the rule just established with MAKE. If they say that they see Pinchy E, sound the word HAVE inserting a long A sound. Say, "HAVE. Is HAVE (long A) a word?" No. Tell the children that sometimes E tags along at the end of a word sound asleep, not making a single sound! This E in HAVE is just going along with the V saying nothing at all. So, you could say that the VE says the sound for V. You would sound and write HAVE like this: H-A-VE. Write on your whiteboard other words that have a sleeping E on the end: HOUSE [H-OU-SE], LIVE [L-I-VE], GIVE [G-I-VE].

Next, display the AN card in your pocket chart and

quickly make new words together: DAN, BAN, JAN, RAN, MAN, CAN, TAN.

WRITING

Play Quick Draw with the AKE words. Then switch to IKE words: MIKE, BIKE, PIKE, HIKE, LIKE. Then OKE words: COKE, JOKE, POKE, WOKE, YOKE. Be sure the children update their journals regularly with new sight words and word families.

Dictate short sentences for them to write: "I have a cat." "We have caps." "We can make it." "Make it now." "He ran fast." "I ran down." "He ran up." "I have to make it." "Jake can make a cake."

CENTERS
Teacher Center:
After reviewing student journals, play a game with your group. You will start and end with the very same word if the game is done right. Call out the word SNAP. Children will write it on their whiteboards, sounding each letter as they write it. Do quick checks of whiteboards as you go.
- Change SNAP to SNIP
- Change SNIP to SLIP
- Change SLIP to SLAP
- Change SLAP to CLAP
- Change CLAP to CLOP
- Change CLOP to CLIP
- Change CLIP to SLIP
- Change SLIP to SLAP
- Change SLAP to SNAP

Start with FLAG
- Change FLAG to FLAP
- FLAP to FLIP
- FLIP to FLOP
- FLOP to CLOP
- CLOP to CLIP
- CLIP to SLIP
- SLIP to SLIM
- SLIM to SLAM
- SLAM to CLAM
- CLAM to CLAP
- CLAP to FLAP
- FLAP to FLAG

Pocket Chart Center:
Making sentences with sight words from Group 5.

Scavenger Hunt:
Children will look for their new sight words in print.

Making Words:
Use R125.

Journal:
Continue daily journaling.

 # Teach Digraphs

OBJECTIVES
1. Child will review letter sounds
2. Child will practice blending & segmenting
3. Child will manipulate sounds to make new words
4. Child will review all sight words
5. Child will learn digraphs SH, TH, WH, CH

MATERIALS
1. SnapWords® learned to date
2. Letters - 6 of each
3. R126-131, 161 (pp. 222-228, 280)
4. Centers, stocked as directed
5. Three sets of pictures on cards - each pair alike (ex: two stars, two hearts, two flowers) for Reading Center)

LESSON
Use R161 to teach or review digraphs. Post the visuals in your classroom if desired, so the children can refer to them. As you introduce each digraph, brainstorm words that start with each one. SH: SHOP, SHIP, SHEET, SHOUT, SHEEP, SHAKE, SHARE, etc. CH: CHIP, CHOP, CHANT, CHIMP, CHEESE, CHAIR, etc. TH: THICK, THREE, THROW, THING, THROAT, and THAT, THOSE, THESE, THERE, THE. WH: WHAT, WHEN, WHERE, WHALE, WHISTLE, WHITTLE, etc. Use R131 for skit directions to reinforce learning digraphs.

WRITING
Start the review by distributing R126 to the class. They can use their whiteboards as desks and should sit in plain view of the classroom wordwall.

SIGHT WORD REVIEW: Say, "Find and write..."

1	said	4	come	7	play	10	jump
2	little	5	want	8	help	11	here
3	make	6	down	9	call	12	call

SOUND REVIEW: Next, ask the children to write the symbol for the sound they hear you say: You will say "By number 1, write Aa. By number 2, write Tt..."

1	A	6	O	11	G	16	W
2	T	7	P	12	L	17	R
3	F	8	M	13	I	18	Y
4	C	9	D	14	B	19	N
5	S	10	H	15	J	20	U

DECODING: Put the children into two groups named the Cougars and the Jaguars (or whatever they want to be called) and alternate questions between the two groups. Show the nonsense words from R127 and have the groups take turns decoding from the cards you hold up.

SEGMENTING
SEGMENTING: Keep the same groups, or make new groups for the segmenting segment. You can name the teams and use tally marks to record points if you wish. You will say a word, then team 1 will segment for you. You will say the next word, and team 2 will segment.

toenail	t-oe-n-ai-l	mailman	m-ai-l-m-a-n
playhouse	p-l-ay-h-ou-se	railroad	r-ai-l-r-oa-d
flagpole	f-l-a-g-p-o-le	mailbox	m-ai-l-b-o-x
plants	p-l-a-n-t-s	trailmix	t-r-ai-l-m-i-x
stripes	s-t-r-i-p-es	package	p-a-ck-a-ge
sandbox	s-a-n-d-b-o-x	treetop	t-r-ee-t-o-p

CENTERS

Comprehension:
Use R128 and have children match sentences to pictures in a way that makes the most sense.

Sentence Unscramble:
Use R129 for this activity, cutting the sentences apart and putting each in a snack baggie ahead of time.

Word Search Center:
Use R130 for this center.

Reading Center:
Children will choose partners when they come to this center by drawing a picture out of the basket. When each child has a picture, they will find their partner by finding a child with exactly the same picture as they have. After each child has had a turn to read a book, put all pictures back in the basket, switch books, and draw new pictures. Repeat until you are out of time.

Writing Center:
Provide paper, envelopes and writing utensils for this center and let the children write letters to give to a classmate, a parent, or you.

Digraphs Center:
Children can look in newspapers or magazines for words beginning with their four digraphs. Have them cut out the words they find, and then arrange them by kind on a paper. They can glue the words in groups, or write them if you prefer.

MORE
For students who are advanced: Provide them with letter cards and sight words. Have them:
1. Form as many words as they can with the letters, writing the words down on blank cards
2. Create sentences using their word cards
3. Place their sentences in the pocket chart to share
4. Illustrate the sentences they write
5. Create their own version of stylized words to share
6. Create a poster together using their words and illustration that goes with their writing

61 as, if, hi

MATERIALS

1. SnapWords® List A Group 5 displayed
2. Resources 131-132 (pp. 228-229)
3. Letter cards for S, C, T, W, H
4. Magazines or newspapers & scissors

ANTICIPATORY SET

Review the SnapWords® from List A Group 5 that you have displayed in your pocket chart by doing activities from your booklet.

Review the digraphs, and depending on the understanding of the children, you might want to take time to let a group of children act out the skit again, using R131.

LESSON - Sight Words AS, IF, HI

Introduce the new sight words for today and quickly relate them each to a similar sight word they already know. AS is like HAS. IF goes with the words IS and IT and IN. HI just stands alone!

Teach AS using the language on the back. The concept of AS is not very simple. In the sentence on the back of the SnapWords® card, AS means "while." Brainstorm other sentences using AS, with you supplying the first few and the children adding some of their own: "I sing as I work." "We talk as we walk." "I laugh as I watch funny movies." We also use AS when we are comparing two different things. "He walks as slow as a turtle." "You're as fast as a bunny!"

Sentences for IF: "See if it is in the box." "Jump over if it is in the way." "See if it is in the mail." "Look and see if it is in your bowl."

HI is a snap. The children will sound Hh and then add the name of the letter I. HI.

WRITING

Review Pinchy E with an auditory/writing game today. First review Pinchy E if you need to, then prompt the children that the first family you will do is AKE. Have them write AKE on their whiteboards. Now, say, "If you put a [sound of Mm] in front of AKE you will have what?" Children should say, MAKE. Say, "Sound it: M-A-KE. Sound and write." Children will sound and write MAKE. Your fingers will be up, four of them, but the final two will be stuck together showing that the E does

not have a sound of his own (See figure 6, page 10). Continue with BAKE, TAKE, LAKE, SHAKE. Now change to OPE. Words: HOPE, MOPE, COPE, LOPE, DOPE. IKE: BIKE, HIKE, LIKE, MIKE. AME: GAME, SAME, TAME, LAME.

CENTERS
Teacher Center:

After reviewing student journals, play a game with your group. You will be saying words and the children will bodyspell the INITIAL sound of the word:

ANT
OCTOPUS
IGLOO
UNDER
UNCLE
INTO
APPLE
OPERA

Now switch to the final sound of the word. Children will listen to the final sound and bodyspell what they hear:

TENT
HOP
HAM
RUNT
MISS
HALF
HAD
DRAG
HALL
CAB

Next, you will play a game using whiteboards. You are going to say a word for them to write. Then the children will add Pinchy E to the end and figure out the new word:

HOP-HOPE
HAT-HATE
TIM-TIME
CUT-CUTE
BAT-BATE
DOT-DOTE
CAP-CAPE

Pocket Chart Center:
Making sentences with sight words from Group 5.

Scavenger Hunt:
Children will look for their new sight words in print.

Sentence Fill in the Blanks:
Use R132.

Journal:
Continue daily journaling.

62 Book 15 - Jip Digs

OBJECTIVES
1. Child will successfully read *Jip Digs*
2. Child will write the story line from dictation
3. Child will correctly sequence events in the story
4. Child will review use of quotation marks
5. Child will review exclamation points

MATERIALS

1. *Jip Digs*, six copies
2. Sentence strips for the book text
3. Books 1-14
4. Resource 133 (p. 230)

ANTicipatory SET

Ask the children how many of them have a puppy at home. If there are children who have a puppy, ask them if their puppy ever digs holes in their yard or does something else their parents might not like very well. If you have a dog of your own, share stories. My dog story from many years ago is about a puppy I had who loved to chew and gnawed all my baby hedge plants off at the ground. Suddenly I had no hedge!

Tell the children you are going to read another story about Jip, the dog famous for tipping, ripping, sipping, nipping and yipping in book 10.

LESSON

The primary focus in this book is the short vowel sound of Ii. Words the children will encounter, that you should hunt for together before you read, are: JIP, DIG, BIG, PIT, DID, WILL.

Using sentence strips, do a search also for how many times you see an exclamation point. Point out that each time you find an exlamation point, it is followed in this story by quotation marks because the exclamation point marks the end of what someone is saying excitedly!

Now read the story line together.

After you have read, ask the children why they think Dad did not want Jip to dig in the back yard. Do they think the boy in the story had a good solution to the problem? What would they have done in his place?

WRITING

The focus for Quick Draw today is vowel sound discrimination. We will soon be focused on the vowel sound for Ee, and many children have problems hearing the difference between Ii and Ee in words. So our goal needs to be to have the children able to easily distinguish between Ii, Oo, Uu, and Aa before adding Ee.

Use these "words" for your game:
JIB, JOB, JAB, JUB.
PAD, PID, POD, PUD.
STUP, STIP, STAP, STOP.
NAB, NIB, NUB, NOB.
PIG, PAG, PUG, POG.
TIP, TAP, TOP, TUP.

Next, say:
Write TIP with an Oo (sound of) (TOP)
TOP with an Aa (TAP)
TAP with a Uu (TUP)

Write TIM with an Oo (TOM)
TOM with an Aa (TAM)
TAM with a Uu (TUM)

Dictate: "Jip can dig and dig." "I can fit in it." "I will see if I can go." "Tim and Jim go up."

CENTERS
Teacher Center:

Review student journals before reading the book for today, making notes of teaching points from the students' writing.

Give each child at the table a copy of the book *Jip Digs*. Read together the cover, title page, and then move to page two. When you have finished, go back to the start and let each child read a page until the book is finished again. From now on, you might want to choose a child to also read the whole book, giving each child a turn on a different day. This way, they will be able to practice fluency by reading the whole story.

Model for the children reading with expression, rather than just a choppy one word at a time. In order to most effectively get the point across, you can read one line with your best expression and have the children echo you.

Reading Center:

Children will read today's book to their partner, then listen along while the other child reads.

Quotation Marks:

Using R133, the children will practice locating what each person has said as the words between the quotation marks, and will color those spoken words yellow. Point out that there are some quotation marks missing! They will need to use their pencils and write them in.

Journal:

Children will write and illustrate their work in their journals.

Pocket Chart:

Review plurals by once again supplying words with an S at the end, written on plain cards for the children to use with their sight words. Ideas: DIGS, SITS, RUNS, TIPS, SIPS, MAKES, LOOKS, SEES, CALLS, WANTS, PLAYS, COMES, HELPS.

Update Skills Tracking form.

Section Three Goals - Lessons 63-77

LEARNER GOALS:

• The child will learn 6 more sounds and their corresponding symbols.

• The child will utilize visuals and motions in recognizing 5 new words on sight.

• The child will successfully read and re-read 7 more books with a focus on fluency.

• The child will learn the following advanced concepts:

ABC order
Past tense of words
Adding "ing"
Final CK ending as in DUCK
R controlled sound spellings
Use of apostrophe to show possession
Use of AN before words starting with a vowel
Pinchy E (final "silent E")
Rhyming
Initial "schwa" sound as in "above"

*/ / means "sounds like what is between slashes.
Ex: A /ah/ means "A sounds like 'ah'."

• The child will engage in comprehension activities

MATERIALS NEEDED FOR SECTION THREE:

• *Alphabet Tales*

• Alphabet Teaching Cards E, V, K, Z, Q, X

• SnapWords® cards for:
(List A, Group 5)

his	back	an	jump	are

• Easy-for-Me™ A Books, numbers 16-22

Wag the Nag
The Vet
Mel's Bell
Ben and Jen
Bill's Mill
Ned and Ted
Meg and Peg

• Resources for Section Three

• Whiteboards, markers, and tube socks as in Section One.

ROOM SET-UP/PREP WORK:

Display the new list of sight words in a pocket chart.

Prepare all resources you will need for Section Three and have them accessible for easy retrieval on the day you will use them.

Photocopy the Skills Tracking form found in Section 3 Resources, one copy per child. Keep these forms in a file or on a clipboard and update regularly.

WORD LISTS & WORD FAMILIES for SECTION 3:

op	im	ess	ed, eg	ag	ig, ug	z, zz
flop	Kim	tress	tred	zag	zig	fizz
slop	trim	chess	Fred	quag	prig	quiz
crop	flim	press	fled	flag	twig	buzz
prop	slim	mess	sled	crag	slug	fuzz
glop	prim	dress	shred	slag	plug	jazz
plop	grim	less	pled	drag	drug	
drop	brim	Bess	bled	brag	glug	
shop	shim	bless	sped	shag	chug	
chop	vim		Greg		shrug	
			keg			

en, un	at	ip	ell	in, ill	ox, ax	am
ken	vat	zip	tell	kin	box	tram
zen	flat	quip	fell	grin	fox	cram
ten	slat	trip	sell	chin	pox	slam
fen	spat	slip	dell	shin	wax	clam
pen	plat	flip	hell	kill	tax	pram
men	drat	clip	bell	quill	sax	dram
den	brat	drip	jell	trill	lax	gram
hen	chat	grip	well	frill	fax	spam
Ben	that	blip	yell	spill	Max	sham
Jen	splat	chip	spell	chill		scram
shun		ship	shell	shrill		

ix, ux	ab	ob, ib	an	ad	um	id, ud
fix	flab	slob	flan	dad	sum	kid
six	crab	glob	clan	glad	slum	quid
mix	slab	blob	span	grad	drum	slid
nix	drab	crib	plan	Brad	glum	grid
tux	blab	glib	gran	Chad	plum	crud
flux			bran	shad	chum	spud
crux			quad			

ub	ot	ap	et, ut	od	it	og
flub	trot	zap	vet	trod	kit	flog
club	slot	trap	wet	dod	zit	clog
slub	plot	flap	fret	prod	quit	grob
drub	blot	slap	whet	plod	flit	blog
grub	spot	clap	glut	shod	slit	
shrub	shot	chap	shut		spit	

63 Ee 👁 his, back, an

OBJECTIVES
1. Child will gain a mental visual of Ee
2. Child will use this visual to recall Ee
3. Child will blend using Ee
4. Child will learn to use AN before a vowel
5. Child will learn sight words HIS, BACK, AN

MATERIALS

1. *Alphabet Tales*, page 87
2. Alphabet Teaching Card for Ee
3. SnapWords® cards HIS, BACK, AN
4. Picture book of animals that hatch
5. Resources 134-135 (pp. 250-251)
6. Word family cards and letters for the blending work:
ED, EG, ET, D, T, R, F, L, S, H, P, B, G, M, W, N, J, Y

ANTICIPATORY SET

Share your picture book with the children to get them excited about the topic of eggs hatching and babies emerging from them. Then ask the children how many of them have painted real Easter eggs before. These eggs are hen eggs that have been cooked. Tell them that today's story is about a girl named Emmy who dearly loved to eat Easter eggs!

STORY

Read the story for Ee and emphasize its sound while you read. Let the children answer the question at the end of the story, and then ask them what they would have done if they were at an egg hunt and found the eggs were all missing!

VISUAL IMPRINTING

Ask the children to close their eyes and imagine seeing Emmy at the egg hunt with her arms reaching out, and her big, long shoe sticking out in the same direction.

BODYSPELLING

uppercase E   lowercase e

Do the motions for E together, using your left hand to make Emmy's back, while your right hand moves twice to make her arms and shoes. Lowercase E is a fist made with left hands so that lowercase E shows at the center.

WRITING

Spend a few minutes saying the sound of Ee. As you say the sound together aloud, the children will bodyspell, then practice forming the letters on their whiteboards.

After the children have practiced writing Ee, dictate these few words for them to sound and write on their whiteboards: END, EFT, EGO, EGRET, ELECT, ELF, ELM, EMBED. (Be sure to have the children carefully sound each sound as they write so they will know how to spell the words. Please avoid using letter names at all.)

Now tell them the Ee sound will move to the inside of the words you will say: NEST, TEST, BEST, BEND, BENT, SENT, BLEND, SPEND, TREND, LEND, WENT, YEN. Use fingermapping (see page 10).

BLENDING

Share R134. Put the word family endings in your pocket chart as before and use the single letters for word beginnings. You will be able to make: TRED, FRED, FLED, SLED, SHRED, PLED, BLED, SPED, GREG, BEG, LEG, MEG, PEG, DREG, WET, FRET, BET, SET, NET, GET, PET, MET, JET, YET. Now that the children have learned Ee, if you have not taught word "vowels," this would be a great time to do so. Show several word cards with all five vowels represented, and have the children pick out the vowel in each one.

CENTERS
Teacher Center:
After reviewing journals, begin the lesson. Today's focus is on discrimination between short E and short I vowel sounds. You will do an oral activity first, where children bodyspell the E or I depending on which one they hear inside the word, then play Quick Draw, making sure to use fingermapping. Use this list of words:

nest	list	mist	legs	prep
trip	slip	bled	grim	fled
clip	sled	tred	trim	film
west	best	lend	grip	bess

Teach sight words, relating HIS to AS, HAS (S with the sound of Z). BACK and AN are easily decoded.

Introduce the use of AN before words beginning with a vowel. You will re-teach in Lesson 64.

Journal Center:
Update with new words, and write daily entry.

Pocket Chart:
Use sight word cards in pocket chart to make sentences.

Scavenger Hunt:
Children can hunt for E words in print.

ACROSS THE CURRICULUM
• **Science** ~ Study the life cycle of an animal that hatches from an egg, such as a chicken or duck. Research animals that lay eggs and collect pictures of them for a class book

• **Math** ~ Review skip counting by 2's and add the concept of a dozen. Show a dozen eggs. Bring in an empty egg carton that has 12 places and have the children collect 12 of something to put in the egg carton to show a dozen.

64 Book 16 - Wag the Nag

MATERIALS

1. *Wag the Nag*, six copies
2. Sentence strips for the book text
3. Books 1-15
4. Resources 136-137 (pp. 252-253)
5. *The Bremen-Town Musicians*

ANTICIPATORY SET

Before reading the book, talk about what a "nag" is. The word nag is used at times in speaking of a small saddle horse or pony, and at other times it refers to a horse that is old and worn out. Read the story *The Bremen-Town Musicians*, which is about animals that had outgrown their usefulness.

LESSON

In today's story, the children will encounter some color words (orange, yellow, and brown). Review all color words as needed, then lead the children in a hunt for the vowel that appears most frequently. See who can identify AG as the primary word family in this book. As you are doing a scan of the story line, draw attention to commas found therein. Model for the children how your voice pauses a bit when there is a comma in the story line.

Read the sentences together. Ask the children what they think they would do if their nag took off with their scarf (or hat). What would they think of to get it back? Do they think the man in the story was smart to do what he did?

WRITING

The focus for Quick Draw today is vowel sound discrimination. Pay close attention to boards when calling out words that have short E and short I sounds in them. Use these words for your game:

BENT, FITS, CAST, COST, CUPS
BAND, SEND, TILT, POND, TWIG,
PEST, WEST, BIBS, GRAD, FIBS
NUT, MOPS, TOPS, BUT, HUTS

Next, say:

Write TOP with an Aa (sound of) (TAP)
TAP with an Ii (TIP)
TIP with a Uu (TUP)
TUP with an Ee (TEP)
Write JIM with an Oo (JOM)

JOM with an Aa (JAM)
JAM with a Uu (JUM)
JUM with an Ee (JEM)
JEM with an Ii (JIM).

Next:
Dictate: "Wag will get the bag." "I will get the rag." "I have a nag." "Wag likes to play." "Wag likes this bag."

CENTERS
Teacher Center:

After reviewing student journals, review the use of AN before words that start with a vowel. Use copy of R136 in a pocket chart, and have the children select A or AN for each one:

ICYCLE, TABLE, ORANGE, APPLE, ALLIGATOR, BALL, BOOK, TOY, OCTOPUS, BACKPACK, UMBRELLA, EGGPLANT, ELEPHANT, TRAY.

Read the book together as usual. Reteach commas on pages 7-8 in the book. Show the children that the comma separates two statements.

Introduce ABC order if you have not done so to date. Use the words you wrote on your whiteboard or chart. Ask the children to find a word that would come at the very beginning of the alphabet (apple, alligator). Model for them how to use the alphabet on the classroom wall to find which letter to search for next. In this case, it will be B (ball, backpack, book). Continue in this way.

Reading Center:
Children will read today's book to their partner, then listen along while the other child reads. Read previous books as there is time.

Pocket Chart:
Using R136, the children will practice choosing AN or A for words provided. They will cut the words apart, then place them in a column. Next, they will put an A or AN card in front of each word. Their results should be recorded in their center folders.

Journal:
Children will write and illustrate their work in their journals.

ABC Order:
Use R137 cut apart and placed in baggies. Children will take the cards out of the baggie and put them into ABC order and then will write the words in order in their center folders.

65 Vv

OBJECTIVES
1. Child will gain a mental visual of Vv
2. Child will use this visual to recall Vv
3. Child will blend using Vv
4. Child will learn past tense shown by -ed
5. Child will review sight words to date

MATERIALS

1. *Alphabet Tales*, page 91
2. Alphabet Teaching Card for Vv
3. Resources 138-139 (pp. 254-255)
4. Picture book about volcanos
5. Letter cards for V, I, A, E(2), M, T, N

ANTICIPATORY SET

Share your picture book with the children to give them a background on volcanos. As always, find out what they already know about volcanos before you start to share.

STORY

Read the story for Vv and this time, ask the children to give you a thumbs up when they hear a word with the Vv sound in it.

VISUAL IMPRINTING

Ask the children to close their eyes and imagine seeing the volcanoes side by side erupting! Ask them what they can "see" in their imaginations. Can they see the lava flowing down the sides of the mountains?

BODYSPELLING

Do the motions for V together, and let the children make their volcano erupting noises! They are going to be able to use the same hand motion for upper and lowercase Vv since the letter is formed the same way for each one.

WRITING

As you say the sound of Vv together aloud, the child(ren) will bodyspell, then practice forming the letters on their whiteboards.
After the children have practiced writing Vv, dictate these few words and nonsense words for them to sound and write on their whiteboards:
VIM, VAT, VENT, EVEN, EVENT, EVA, OVA, MAV, FIV, STIV, SHIV, PLAV.
Dictate: "A vet has a vat for his pet."
"Eva got in the van to go."
"I see a vent in a van even."

BLENDING

Share R138. There really is no word family today for blending Vv, so you will be using the letter cards to build the words listed below. Say the word, sound the word, then select the letters you will need with the children prompting you.
VIM, VAT, VENT, EVEN, EVENT, EVA, VAN

CENTERS
Teacher Center:

After reviewing journals, begin the lesson. Today's lesson will focus on making words past tense. For today, we will be using only words that truly just add the ED at the end rather than on words that change for past tense, such as RUN to RAN.
You will need to stress the fact that the children will NOT always be able to hear the past tense sounding like ED. Sometimes, past tense sounds like Dd and sometimes like Tt. They will need to rely on making sense of the idea of past tense from the context of the sentence. Your teaching activity will reflect this. Write the words or display them on cards in your pocket chart:
KICK, SAND, HAND, LICK, VENT, WANT, LOCK, TILT, FOLD, LOOK, COOK, LAND, FILL, YELL, LIFT. Decode the words together and point out that these words are all things we can do. If we are going to do them, we write or say the word just as they appear on the cards. If we have already done the thing we are talking about, we will add an ED on the end. SAY:
"I will kick the ball." "I kicked the ball [aleady did it]."
"I will sand the bat." "I sanded the bat."
"I will hand it to Dad." "I handed it to Dad."
"I will lick my candy." "I licked my candy."
"I will vent the van." "I vented the van." *(opened windows to air it out)*
"I want to go." "I wanted to go."
"I will lock up." "I locked up."
"Jip will tilt it." "Jip tilted it."
"I will fold this." "I folded this."
"I will look for Pat." "I looked for Pat."
"I will cook this." "I cooked this."
"The jet will land." "The jet landed."
"I will fill the glass." "I filled the glass."
"I will yell for you." "I yelled for you."
"I can lift this." "I lifted this."

Journal Center:
Update with new words, and write daily entry.

Pocket Chart:
Use SnapWords® cards in pocket chart to make sentences. Add some of the words above so the children can practice their past tense.

Past Tense Practice:
Use R139 for practice in past tense.

ACROSS THE CURRICULUM
• Science ~ Study volcanos.

66 jump, are

OBJECTIVES
1. Child will learn sight words JUMP, ARE
2. Child will learn concept of R-controlled vowels
3. Child will practice R-controlled ending (er)
4. Child will review ABC order
5. Child will review sight words

MATERIALS

1. SnapWords® Cards for JUMP, ARE
2. Resource 135,140 (pp. 251, 256)
3. Large cards with a vowel on each one
4. Cards for AR, B, C, D, H, F, J, L, M, P, R, S, T

ANTICIPATORY SET

Remind the children of the story of Pinchy E they acted out. Today there will be a new skit called "Bossy R and the Vowels." Say, "Bossy R was the sort of fellow who talked all the time and told everyone what to do. Have you known anyone like him? Today we are going to act out the story of Bossy R." Choose five children to be the five vowels. Choose a child to be Bossy R. Each child who is a vowel will hold a card with their letter written on it.

LESSON - Sight Words JUMP, ARE

Line the vowel children up, then say, "One day on the playground, Bossy R told the vowels that they were not allowed to talk and say their own sounds anymore. If he was around, standing right by them, they were to not say anything at all. HE was going to do the talking! Four of the vowels were so afraid of Bossy R that they decided they would do exactly as he said!" Have Vowel E and Bossy R stand by each other. Write the word HER on your whiteboard. Say, "Do you see your friends in this word?" Draw attention to the E and the R in HER. "Let's see if the E is going to do what Bossy R said." Sound out HER: H-ER. Say, "How many sounds did you hear? Only two. The Hhh and the Rrrr sound! Sounds like E was afraid to speak!" Repeat the process with OR using the word WORM sounded out like: W-OR-M. Use FUR; F-UR. Use SHIRT; SH-IR-T. Next, put A and Bossy R next to each other and say, "Vowel A was not so easy to boss around. When it came time for them to speak, A didn't speak, but he did pinch Bossy R and Bossy R was so startled that instead of saying his normal sound [er], he shouted his name! AR!" Use the words CAR, FAR, TAR. Next show the sight word ARE and point out that the R is really big in the center. Ask the children if they can hear anything other than R saying his name? Briefly use the ARE in sentences. "Are you ready?"

Briefly, now, share the sight word JUMP and point out that it is a decodable word. Ask the children what JUMP would become if you replaced the J with a B? [bump], a D? [dump], an H? [hump], an L? [lump] an M? [mump], a P? [pump], an R? [rump], and an S? [sump].

WRITING

Play Quick Draw first with the UMP family of words: JUMP, BUMP, DUMP, HUMP, LUMP, MUMP, PUMP, RUMP, SUMP, STUMP, PLUMP.

Have the children close their eyes now, and imagine seeing the SnapWord image for ARE. Ask, "Where is the R in this word? At the beginning, the middle or the end?" Have the children open their eyes and write ARE from memory.

Next, tell the children the words you are going to use have Vowel A and Bossy R in them. Use: CAR, FAR, TAR, BAR, MAR, JAR, STAR, DART, PART, CART, TART, START. Finally use ARM, ARMY, ART.

Dictate: "I can not jump in the car!"
"I will jump by the jar." "I will not jump on the dart."

BLENDING

Put the AR card and all the individual letters in your pocket chart. You will be able to make the words you practiced writing. CAR, FAR, TAR, STAR, JAR, BAR, DART, PART, CART, TART, START, SMART.

CENTERS
Teacher Center:

After reviewing journals, begin the lesson. Today's focus is on R controlled vowels. Children will need R140 and a yellow crayon. In addition, write the words from the chart below on 3x5" cards to display in the pocket chart. In the first four columns, the yellow will indicate that the R is saying his normal sound: [er]. In the fifth column, the R is being pinched and is saying his name [AR].

worm	her	burn	stir	start
work	fern	curl	fir	party
word	silver	hurt	first	smart
world	herd	turn	shirt	cart

Next, focus on R140. Children will find every instance in which a vowel is followed by Bossy R, and they will color the pair yellow. Practice reading the sentences.

Journal Center:
Update with new words, and write daily entry.

Pocket Chart:
Use sight words and Bossy R words in pocket chart to make sentences.

Scavenger Hunt:
Children can hunt for Bossy R words in print and sort by vowel sound.

OBJECTIVES
1. Child will successfully read *The Vet*
2. Child will write the story line from dictation
3. Child will review ABC order
4. Child will review use of quotation marks
5. Child will review R controlled vowels

MATERIALS

1. *The Vet*, six copies
2. Sentence strips for the book text
3. Books 1-16
4. Resources 141-142 (pp. 257-258)
5. Information about vets, or book about taking a pet to a vet

ANTICIPATORY SET

Before reading the book, talk about what a vet is, what he or she does, and find out if the children have ever been to a vet's office. Have a bit of sharing time to find out what the children already know about vets.

Next, share with the children that a word that rhymes with vet is JET. In the story for today, a girl says, "I bet I will jet." Of course, she is not talking about taking off in a jet. Rather, she just means, "I think I will get out of here!"

LESSON

The prominent word family today, of course, is ET. Do a search through the sentence strips for the ET words. Next draw attention to the words that are inside quotation marks and ask the child to watch for who is talking when you get to that part of the story.

Read the sentences together. When you have finished, ask the children what they think the vet was doing with the pet raccoon. Do they think the pet was hurt in some way? Do they think the raccoon thought he was going to go fishing in the barrel of water, or did he fall in accidentally.

WRITING

The focus for Quick Draw today is the reinforcement of Bossy R concept.

You will need to alert the children to which vowel you will be using in your lists of words because if R truly is being bossy, they will not be able to hear the vowels! Be sure to use fingermapping when you sound out the words, and be sure to have two fingers touching to represent two letters in the word making one sound together [er, or, ur, or ir].

worm	her	burn	stir	start
work	fern	curl	fir	party
word	silver	hurt	first	smart
world	herd	turn	shirt	cart

If you have a big book that has a lot of R controlled words in it, share it with the children so you can find the words that fall into this category. It will be important for the children to understand that Bossy R only is bossy when he has to follow behind a vowel. In the word RUN or RADIO, he is not bossy because he is already first!

Now dictate: "My burn will hurt."
"The girl is first."
"The worm can not work."
"Will you start the party?"

CENTERS

Teacher Center:

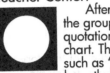

After reviewing student journals, have the group work with you to generate short quotations to write on your whiteboard or flip chart. They can each give you one sentence, such as "I said, 'Stop it now!'" When you have their sentences recorded, show them that when you are identifying what someone is saying, it is like you are cupping your hands around their words. Cup your hands around the words in the first sentence, and tell the children that these are the words someone actually said.

Use R141 and guide the children through identifying the quote.

Read the book for today, letting each child have a turn to read. Focus on expression, and echo read if you feel it is needful.

Reading Center:
Children will read today's book to their partners, and then listen along while the other child reads. Read previous books as time permits.

Pocket Chart:
Using R141, the children will practice identifying quotes. They will color the words spoken with yellow and underline who said the words with another color.

Journal:
Children will write and illustrate their work in their journals.

ABC Order:
Use R142 cut apart and placed in baggies. Children will take the cards out of the baggie and put them into ABC order and then will write the words in order in their center folders.

OBJECTIVES
1. Child will successfully read *Mel's Bell*
2. Child will write the story line from dictation
3. Child will learn the possessive [as in Mel's]
4. Child will review use of quotation marks
5. Child will review R controlled vowels

MATERIALS

1. *Mel's Bell*, six copies
2. Sentence strips for the book text
3. Books 1-17
4. R142 (reduced)-R143 (pp. 258-259)
5. Book *The Lion and the Mouse*

ANTICIPATORY SET

Read the book, *The Lion and the Mouse* about how a tiny mouse gnaws through a rope net to free a huge lion. The obvious point to the story is that even though a mouse is very small compared to a lion, he can be strong enough to free a captured lion from a hunter's net. Tell the children that today they will need to watch for another mouse that gnawed through a rope, and will need to tell you at the end of the story, where that rope was.

LESSON

The prominent word families today are EL and ELL. Do a search through the sentence strips for those words. As you are going, point out the apostrophe in the title and on page 2, and teach the children that that tiny mark before the final S means that the bell belongs to Mel.

Next draw attention to the words that are inside quotation marks and ask the child to watch for who is talking when you get to that part of the story.

Read the sentences together. When you have finished, ask the children what they think the mouse gnawed through? If they cannot guess, they certainly will when they are at Teacher Center!

WRITING

The focus for Quick Draw today is the use of the double LL at the end of the ELL and ILL families, as well as discrimination between short E and I sounds. Use the words found below to play your game, mixing up the order so the children have to decide if they are hearing an E or an I:

bell	dell	yell	still	mill
Nell	smell	jell	spill	drill
sell	spell	Bill	trill	fill
tell	fell	sill	grill	hill

Dictate: "Nell will sell the bell."
"Bill will fill the mill."
"He will spill the dill."
"I will yell for Nell."

CENTERS
Teacher Center:

After reviewing student journals, read the book for today, reminding the children to look for something they think a mouse gnawed through. They will also be looking for an apostrophe showing that something belongs to a person.

When you have read the book, generate short sentences with your group, using each of their names. You go first, then let the children take turns while you write what they say. The point is to use the possessive tense. Tell them they will each need to think of two things: 1- the name of a person, and 2- a thing.
"This is Mrs. Smith's book."
"It is Ron's ball."
"That is Jen's backpack."
etc.

Reading Center:
Children will read today's book to their partners, and then listen along while the other child reads. Read previous books as time permits.

Pocket Chart:
Children will make up sentences using sight words, but including also possessive tense. Use blank notecards and let the children write their own name with an apostrophe S at the end. Then they should record their sentences in their center folders.

Journal:
Children will write and illustrate their work in their journals.

Word Sort:
Use R142 cut apart and placed in baggies. Children will take the cards out of the baggie and sort them under the right Bossy R/Vowel team.

ACROSS THE CURRICULUM
• Math ~ Use R143 and teach the concept of bar graphs. Use the same words to teach tally marks.

OBJECTIVES
1. Child will successfully read *Ben and Jen*
2. Child will write the story line from dictation
3. Child will review the possessive [as in Mel's]
4. Child will review use of quotation marks
5. Child will practice rhyming

MATERIALS

1. *Ben and Jen* six copies
2. Sentence strips for the book text
3. Books 1-18
4. Resource 144 (p. 260)
5. Book about bears
6. A big book of rhymes

ANTicipatory SET

Ask the children what they know about bears, then share with them your book about bears. Discuss with the children the fact that sometimes animals look really scary when maybe they are friendly and nice. The problem is we don't always know, so we have to be very careful and be safe when we are around animals that we don't know. Tell them that in the story today, a bear seemed pretty scary to a hen named Jen.

LESSON
The prominent word family today is EN. Do a scan of the sentence strips for these words. Next, find the apostrophes that show possession (pages 5 and 8), the use of exclamation points to show strong emotion (pages 4-6 and 8). Finally, do a scan for quotation marks (page 6).

Read the story together and model reading with expression and phrasing for fluency. When you have finished reading, ask the children to scan the sentence strips looking for pairs of words that rhyme. In this book many of them will end in EN.

Display your big book of rhymes and practice finding the rhyming pairs in the book. Draw attention to the ends of the words to look for identical spellings.

WRITING
The focus for Quick Draw today is the EN word family and vowel discrimination. Use the words provided in the chart, and use fingermapping as you play.

Jen	then	past	flag	sand
Ben	west	shop	chip	path
ten	step	cast	clap	went
men	sift	rift	slat	rest
den	bust	rust	must	tusk
pen	best	test	chop	slip

Dictate: "Jen has a pen and Ben has a den."
"Ten men slip and trip."
"The test is the best."
"The chap will clap for Hap."

CENTERS
Teacher Center:

After reviewing student journals, read the book for today, reminding the children to look for quotes, apostrophes and exclamation points. Model reading fluency for them, using phrasing and good expression. Let them echo you, a page at a time.

When you have finished reading, play a game in which you say a word and each child in turn says a word that rhymes with your word. Ideas are given for your use should you need to prompt the children:
JEN: [BEN, MEN, TEN, PEN, DEN, THEN]
PIT: [BIT, KIT, MIT, HIT, FIT, SIT, LIT]
FLOP: [STOP, POP, HOP, TOP, COP, SHOP, CHOP]
ZIP: [TRIP, SLIP, CLIP, SNIP, TIP, NIP, DRIP, GRIP]
BIG: [FIG, WIG, RIG, TWIG, DIG, ZIG]
CAT: [HAT, RAT, CHAT, THAT, BRAT, SPLAT]

Reading Center:
Children will read today's book to their partners, and then listen along while the other child reads. Read previous books as time permits.

Pocket Chart:
Children will make up sentences using sight words. Supply blank cards for the children to write rhyming words on so they can use them in sentence building. Put an example sentence in the top row as a model for them:
"The bat is on the hat."
"Pam likes spam and ham."
"Ed fed the red hen."
"I want to play with Ben and Jen."
If you would like to, you could write the letters that make the words rhyme in a contrasting color.

Journal:
Children will write and illustrate their work in their journals.

Sentence Building:
Use R144. Children will continue to practice rhyming and sentence building.

ACROSS THE CURRICULUM
•Science ~ Study brown bears. See the following websites:
http://kids.nationalgeographic.com/kids/animals/creaturefeature/brown-bear/
http://www.wildlife.alaska.gov/index.cfm?adfg=bears.trivia
http://www.adfg.state.ak.us/pubs/notebook/biggame/brnbear.php

70 Kk

OBJECTIVES
1. Child will gain a mental visual of Kk
2. Child will blend using Kk
3. Child will learn CK sound spelling
4. Child will review "Pinchy E"
5. Child will review digraphs

MATERIALS

1. *Alphabet Tales*, page 95
2. Alphabet Teaching Card for Kk
3. R135, 145-147 (pp. 251, 261-263)
4. Pictures of items that start with Kk
5. Letter cards for ACK, ECK, ICK, OCK, UCK, B, D, H, J, L, M, R, S, T, W, Y, A, O, U, E, I
6. Story books with many words containing CK

ANTICIPATORY SET
Ask the children how many of them have played a game in which they had to kick a ball. It might be soccer, football, or even a made-up game. Show the children that when you kick your leg out, sometimes your arm goes up to help balance you (your body is forming a K when you do that). In today's story we are going to see how two kids used their kicks to help out a friend!

STORY

Read the story for Kk and at the end of the reading, ask the children to stand up right where they are and make their bodies form a whole-body K. Their backs are nice and straight, they will have one leg out and one arm raised.

VISUAL IMPRINTING

Ask the children to close their eyes and imagine seeing Kyle and Katie with their arms out and their legs kicking. Are their backs on the left or on the right?

BODYSPELLING

Do the motions for K together, and let the children say, "I kick a ball and fly a kite" pretending their outstretched arm is holding a kite string!

WRITING

As you say the sound of Kk together aloud, the children will bodyspell, then practice forming the letters on their whiteboards. Use the belly button as the point at which the arm and leg emerge, one going up at a slant, the other going down at a slant.

After the children have practiced writing Kk, dictate these few words and nonsense words for them to sound and write on their whiteboards: KIM, KEG, KEN, KIN, KID, KIT. Remind the children of the Pinchy E who lurks at the end of words waiting to pinch unsuspecting vowels. Tell them that in the next words, Pinchy E is up to his tricks again and although they cannot hear him, they will need to be sure and write him! If they hear the Kk sound, it will be a K, not a C:

KITE, KATE, TAKE, MAKE, RAKE, SAKE, FLAKE, SNAKE, BAKE, BRAKE, LAKE, MIKE, BIKE, HIKE, LIKE, PETE, WOKE, JOKE

BLENDING

Share R145. Use letters: K, I, M, E, G, N, D, T to blend the words: KIM, KEG, KEN, KIN, KID, KIT.
Next, use an E at the end for Pinchy E and blend these: KITE, KATE, TAKE, MAKE, RAKE and the other words used in the writing exercise.

CENTERS
Teacher Center:

After reviewing journals, begin the lesson. Today's lesson will teach the CK sound spelling. Briefly teach the concept that when C and K go walking together, they just say one sound: the Kk sound they learned for both C and K. Using the books you gathered for this purpose, have the children browse the text looking for CK words.

In the chart below you will find words ending in CK utilizing all five vowels. Display one ending at a time and have the children go through the alphabet to figure out how many words they can make using each ending.

ack	eck	ick	ock	uck
back	beck	kick	dock	buck
hack	neck	pick	hock	duck
lack	deck	lick	jock	luck
Jack	peck	sick	lock	muck
Mack	fleck	tick	rock	suck
tack	speck	nick	sock	tuck
sack		wick	tock	yuck
rack		Dick	stock	snuck
stack		hick	shock	stuck

Journal Center:
Update with new words, and write daily entry.

Pocket Chart:
Use sight words in pocket chart to make sentences. Add some CK words on plain cards for use in this group.

Sentence/Picture Match:
Use R146.

71 Zz

OBJECTIVES
1. Child will gain a mental visual of Zz
2. Child will blend using Zz and ZZ
3. Child will review CK sound spelling
4. Child will blend with "Pinchy E"
5. Child will learn A /uh/ as in ABOUT

MATERIALS

1. *Alphabet Tales*, page 99
2. Alphabet Teaching Card for Zz
3. Resources 148-149 (pp. 264-265)
4. Pictures of items that start with Zz
5. Plain letter cards for AZE, A, C, E, F, G, H, I, J, L, M, P, R, S, T, ZZ
6. Story book about lightning

ANTicipatory SET

Ask the children what they know about lightning. Have they been in a storm where they could see the lightning striking in the distance? Let them share their thoughts and experiences about lightning, then share your book with them.

STORY

Read the story for Zz and at the end of the reading, ask the children if they thought Mr. Luther's idea was a good one. Ask if they thought some kids at the fair might have felt the the lightning was their helper and not something to be afraid of in this story.

VISUAL IMPRINTING

Ask the children to close their eyes and imagine seeing the zigs and zags of the lighting. Have them air-spell the Zz they are seeing in their minds, making sure to start on the left and move to the right to start with. They will be able to feel the shape of Z if they hold up their right hand and stretch their arm left across the front of their body as they are in position to start writing the letter. They will make a table to the right, then slide left and down, then finish with another table.

BODYSPELLING

Do the motions for Z together, pointing out that their left hand makes a slide that does not move, while their right hand is a table that is first on top, then on the bottom of the slide.

WRITING

As you say the sound of Zz together aloud, the children will bodyspell, then practice forming the letters on their whiteboards. First they will make a table going to the right, then without lifting their marker, they will slide down and end

up under the starting point of the table....then finish with a nice flat table on the bottom.

After the children have practiced writing Zz, dictate these few words for them to write on their whiteboards: ZAG, ZIP, ZIG, ZIT, ZAP, ZEN.

Next, they will double the final Z: FIZZ, BUZZ, FUZZ, JAZZ.

Next, the children will be using Pinchy E again: HAZE, LAZE, SIZE, CRAZE, FAZE, FROZE.

BLENDING

Share R148. Use letter cards to blend the AZE words: HAZE, LAZE, CRAZE, FAZE.

Blend the ZZ words next: FIZZ, BUZZ, FUZZ, JAZZ.

Next, blend ZAG, ZIP, ZIG, ZIT, ZAP, ZEN. Although the children have already sounded and spelled these words, blending from letter cards will give them another opportunity to make words using a different approach: visual and auditory, leaving out the kinesthetic element.

CENTERS
Teacher Center:

After reviewing journals, begin the lesson. Today's lesson will teach the schwa: the initial a that sounds like UH. Tell the children it sounds like the sound a person might make when they are trying to think of something... "Uhh." Although the schwa can be spelled with other vowels, we focus only on the initial A in this lesson. Words to share with the children are these:

ago	about	away	again	another
around	across	above	along	annoy
attend	ability	amaze	astound	attempt

Journal Center:
Update with new words, and write daily entry.

Pocket Chart:
Use sight words in pocket chart to make sentences. Add some Z and ZZ words on plain cards for use in this group.

Sentence/Picture Match:
Use R149.

ACROSS THE CURRICULUM
• Science ~ Study lightning.
http://www.kidslightning.info/zaphome.htm
http://www.howstuffworks.com/lightning.htm
http://content.scholastic.com/browse/article.
jsp?id=4915

72))) 👂 📖 Qu

OBJECTIVES
1. Child will gain a mental visual of Qu
2. Child will blend using Qu
3. Child will decode words with Qu
4. Child will blend Qu with "Pinchy E"
5. Child will review all sight words learned

MATERIALS

1. *Alphabet Tales*, page 103
2. Alphabet Teaching Card for Qq
3. Resources 150-51 (pp. 266-267)
4. Plain letter cards for QU, I, T, C, E, LL, L, K, P, D, A
5. Coins, including quarters

ANTICIPATORY SET

Discuss with the children the places we should be extra quiet, and which places we can be as loud as we want to be. Share with the children that sometimes people are very shy and so when they are around people they tend to be very quiet. Other people are not shy and they just talk to anyone. Our story today is about a boy who was very shy and quiet, and how he learned to make a lot of noise!

STORY

Read the story for Qq and at the end of the reading, ask the children if they can think of times or places where they felt very shy and didn't want to talk. How did they feel? What made them feel comfortable enough to start talking again?

VISUAL IMPRINTING

Ask the children to close their eyes and see the quiet pool that Quentin swam in. Can they see the diving board? Which side is it on? The right side or the left? What other letter looks something like the Q? (O) How are they the same? How are they different?

BODYSPELLING

Do the motions for Q together, pointing out that their left hand makes the round pool, while their right pointer finger makes the diving board. In lowercase Q, the left hand opens wide up and the right hand makes the curve.

WRITING

As you say the sound of Qq together aloud, the children will bodyspell, then practice forming the letters on their whiteboards. Before writing any more, remind the children about the story, and how Quentin didn't like to go anywhere without Uncle Ule. Tell them that to this day, Q does not go anywhere without the U. If they find a Q in a word, the very next letter will always be a U. Say the sound of Qu for the children (KWUH) and let them practice, then write the Qu.

Dictate these few words for them to write on their whiteboards: QUIT, QUICK, QUIET, QUILL, QUILT, QUACK, QUID, QUIP, QUELL. You will need to remind them of the special endings in some of these words: LL and CK.

Now dictate these sentences:
"Now I will quit."
"Quin Fin has a big grin."
"Mom's quilt will wilt in the sun."
"Quick! Lick the stick!"

BLENDING

Share R150. Put all the letters in your pocket chart and build one letter at a time for the children to decode. Use these words:

QUACK, QUILL, QUILT, QUIT, QUIET, QUID, QUICK, QUELL, QUIP.

Find the sight words QUIT and QUICK in the back of the book and talk about the words with the children. Have them use the words in sentences orally.

Before breaking into centers, using the List A Group 5 words turned to the plain side, and using the classroom wall, do a quick review playing the Find and Write game.

CENTERS
Teacher Center:

After reviewing journals, begin the lesson. Today's lesson will revisit the role of Pinchy E at the end of a word. Display the first word in each pair and work through with the children what the new word would be once Pinchy E is added:

quit	quite		cut	cute
mad	made		Sid	side
tap	tape		rid	ride
cot	cote		tot	tote
rot	rote		not	note
cod	code		rip	ripe
rat	rate		pat	pate
bit	bite		cap	cape

Journal Center:
Update with new words, and write daily entry.

Pocket Chart:
Use sight words in pocket chart to make sentences. Add the new QU words on plain cards: QUIT, QUICK, QUIET.

Sentence/Picture Match:
Use R 151.

73 Xx

OBJECTIVES
1. Child will gain a mental visual of Xx
2. Child will blend using Xx
3. Child will decode words with Xx
4. Child will practice ABC order
5. Child will review sight words List A

MATERIALS

1. *Alphabet Tales*, page 107
2. Alphabet Teaching Card for Xx
3. Resources 152-154 (pp. 268-270)
4. Pictures of items that contain an Xx
5. Plain letter cards for IX, AX, OX, UX, B, F, P, W, T, S, L, M, N, C, R
6. A book about the benefits of exercise

ANTICIPATORY SET

Discuss with the children some good forms of exercise. What do they like to do for exercise? Let them share their preferences, then begin a discussion about the value of regular exercise for the body. Share the book you selected for this purpose.

Now tell the childern that today's story is about some boys that found that getting extra exercise helped them do some things they had not been able to do before!

STORY

Read the story for Xx and at the end of the reading, practice the X sound together. Show the children that it is like putting CKS together as in kiCKS, or triCKS.

VISUAL IMPRINTING

Ask the children to close their eyes and see the boys getting their extra exercise. What do they look like? Can they do that same thing with their bodies? Let the children stand up and make an X with their whole body as they say, "I am getting extra exercise!"

BODYSPELLING

Do the motion for X together, and point out that the same motion does for both upper and lowercase letters. The lowercase X is just a bit smaller.

WRITING

As you say the sound of Xx together aloud, the children will bodyspell, then practice forming the letters on their whiteboards. Play Quick Draw with the following lists of words. Prompt the children to listen carefully for the correct vowels to use in their words.

Dictate these words for them to write on their whiteboards: BOX, FOX, POX, WAX, TAX, SAX, LAX, FAX, MAX, FIX, SIX, MIX, NIX, TUX, FLUX, CRUX.
Now dictate these sentences:
"I see a fox on the box."
"Max will send me a fax."
"I will mix six."
"The sax is by the ax."

BLENDING

Share R152. Put all the letters in your pocket chart and build one word at a time for the children to decode. Use these words:

BOX, FOX, POX, WAX, TAX, SAX, LAX, FAX, MAX, FIX, SIX, MIX, NIX, TUX, FLUX, CRUX.

Put BOX in the pocket chart and have the children blend the sounds into a word. Next, ask what would have to change to make the word say FOX. Continue in this way.

CENTERS
Teacher Center:

After reviewing journals, begin the lesson. Today's lesson will revisit ABC order. Use the words below (see R153) and offer support as you guide the children into putting the word cards into ABC order. Do one column at a time:

at	big	and	are	by
call	come	back	but	his
did	has	can	do	my
help	little	down	for	not
jump	ran	get	go	out
like	this	have	here	see
said	up	it	make	this
want	we	look	now	you

Journal Center:
Update with new words, and write daily entry.

Pocket Chart:
Use sight words in pocket chart to make sentences. Add the new X words on plain cards: FOX, BOX, FIX, MIX, SIX.

ABC Order:
Use R154.

ACROSS THE CURRICULUM
•**Health** - Study the effects of getting regular exercise on our body.
•**Science** - Study the heart and how it works to keep the body alive.

Book 20 - Bill's Mill

OBJECTIVES
1. Child will successfully read *Bill's Mill*
2. Child will write the story line from dictation
3. Child will review the possessive [as in Bill's]
4. Child will review all sounds learned
5. Child will review sound spellings

MATERIALS

1. *Bill's Mill,* six copies
2. Sentence strips for the book text
3. Books 1-19
4. Resources 155-156 (pp. 271-275)
5. Fresh or dried dill, dill pickles

ANTICIPATORY SET

Let the children smell the dill you brought and share with them that this herb is one way dill pickles are flavored. Ask the children if they like dill pickles, and would enjoy sampling a tiny bite of one?

The story today is about a man named Bill who grew dill in his yard, and he also has a mill. Explain that mills run by water running over the wheel and that wheel turns a gear inside the mill where grain is ground into flour.

LESSON

The prominent word family today is ILL. Do a scan of the sentence strips for the many ILL words. Point out the apostrophe in the title and review the idea of possessions. The mill belongs to Bill. See if the children can find the other apostrophe in the text.

Read the story together and once again, model reading with expression and phrasing for fluency. When you have finished reading, ask the children to quickly call out pairs of rhyming words (just two each).

WRITING

The focus for Quick Draw today is the ILL word family and also the review of sound spellings the children have learned in these lessons. Use the words provided in the chart, and use fingermapping as you play. As you come to each sound spelling, do a quick reminder of how to spell the sound:

Bill	fill	gill	sill	still
trill	look	book	took	brook
cook	cow	now	how	brown
frown	clown	out	shout	clout
cloud	snow	blow	crow	slow
you	soup	group	are	bar
far	car	star	part	her
over	under	worm	work	word
curl	turn	fur	stir	skirt
shirt	dirt	bird	girl	first

CENTERS

Teacher Center:

After reviewing student journals, continue to practice words with the sound spellings provided in the writing portion of the lesson.

Next, give the children the third Lily Pad game (R155) and practice quickly finding each sound.

The fourth Lily Pad game will be used to review sound spellings that have more than one letter (p. 273).

Reading Center:
Children will read today's book to their partners, and then listen along while the other child reads. Read previous books as time permits.

Pocket Chart:
Children will make up sentences using sight words. Supply blank cards for the children to write their name on using an apostrophe S so they can use their own name in a sentence. Put an example sentence at the top of the pocket chart:
"Don's bat wants to play with me."
"Mom said to make Bill's bed."
"I like Pam's little cat."
"Come and help me make Sam's bed."

Journal:
Children will write and illustrate their work in their journals.

Sentence Unscramble:
Use R156.

OBJECTIVES
1. Child will successfully read *Ned and Ted*
2. Child will write the story line from dictation
3. Child will learn to read and write -ING
4. Child will review all sight words learned
5. Child will review sound spellings

MATERIALS

1. *Ned and Ted,* six copies
2. Sentence strips for the book text
3. Books 1-20
4. Resource 157

ANTICIPATORY SET

Ask the children if they can think of anyone who was a bit on the rowdy side? What are some of the things that person might do to make you believe he or she is rowdy? Are they ever rowdy? Ask the children if they think their mom ever just wants them to go to sleep at night so she can get a bit of quiet? Tell the children that there are twins in this book who got a bit rowdy and finally got sent to bed!

LESSON

The prominent word family today is ED. Do a scan of the sentence strips for the ED words. Find the "Shhh" on page 8 and have the children practice doing this for a second. Ask the children to find the apostrophe (page 8).

Read the story together and be sure to express emotion when you get to a sentence that ends in an exclamation point!

When you have read the story, talk about how the story uses the words FED and LED. Did the boys really do that or does FED really mean "throw food at?" Does LED really mean "drag and push?"

WRITING

The focus for Quick Draw today is the ED word family and also the review of sound spellings. Again, as you come to each sound spelling, do a quick reminder of how to spell the sound. Start with "led" and go from left to right.

led	bed	fled	sped	tred
sled	when	then	Ben	bent
sent	enter	bend	fill	still
mill	will	spill	spell	well
bell	sell	smell	work	word
worm	curl	fur	turn	burn
girl	sir	dirt	shirt	bird
park	stark	star	Bart	start
mart	mall	ball	stall	tall
her	fern	silver	herd	nerd

CENTERS
Teacher Center:

After reviewing student journals, introduce the use of ING at the end of words. First tell the children that we use ING when we are talking about things we do. Give the examples: COOKING, LOOKING, RESTING, NESTING, PLAYING, JUMPING, SEEING, WANTING.

Ask the children to give you some ING words to write on your board. Invariably, the children will come up with some words that will need a double letter before adding ING. The explanation for this is that the I in ING will pinch the vowel unless there are TWO letters between him and the vowel. For instance: TAP would turn into TAPE if the ING were added without doubling the P -- TAPING instead of TAPPING.

In the examples given in the first paragraph, all the words either had a double vowel in the middle, or they had two consonants before the ING was added. This concept of doubling the final consonant will need to be revisited frequently.

Use these words to add ING and provide guidance if the children need any. Otherwise, ask them to talk together about whether or not the words need another consonant before adding ING or not. Use these words:

CUT, RUN, SIT, TROT, SPOT, SHOP, STOP, TRIM, FLAG, SLED, DRAG, PLUG, CHAT, SLIP, CLIP, DRIP, CHIP. All these words need to have the final consonant doubled before adding the ING. The reason is that the vowel is alone and unprotected by a buddy letter.

Add ING to these words (no double letter required): SPEND, SEND, TILT, WILT, BARK, JUMP, LIFT, SIFT, HELP, BACK, ASK, VENT.

Reading Center:
Children will read today's book to their partners. After reading today's book, have the children pair up to review their sight words.

Pocket Chart:
Children will make up sentences using sight words. Supply blank cards for the children to write an ING word on to use in their sentence. Display a model sentence or two:
"Pam is sitting down."
"Mom is sending me out."
"I am not falling down."
"The kids are playing now."

Journal:
Children will write and illustrate their work in their journals.

Fill in the Blank:
Use R157. The children will use the words in the word bank, will add ING to them, and use them to fill in the blanks in the sentences given.

OBJECTIVES
1. Child will successfully read *Meg and Peg*
2. Child will write the story line from dictation
3. Child will review the use of -ING
4. Child will review all sight words learned
5. Child will review sound spellings
6. Child will describe characters

MATERIALS

1. *Meg and Peg,* six copies
2. Sentence strips for the book text
3. Books 1-21
4. Resources 158-160 (pp. 277-279)
5. Story *The Ant and the Grasshopper*

ANTICIPATORY SET

Read the story of the Ant and the Grasshopper. When you have finished, let the children share their impressions of the characters. Ask them how they would describe each character. Do they know someone that just likes to play and not ever do his chores? Do they also know someone who is really good at taking care of his chores? The story today is about two hens; one who just wanted to play, and the other who did her work.

LESSON
Before you read, find the QU words and make sure the children can decode them or recognize them on sight. Practice decoding EGG. Make sure the children can read TWO. Ask the children to find a word that ends in ING. (page 6).

Read the story line together, modeling good reading expression.

When you are finished, ask the children what they think of Meg and Peg. Did they think Peg learned a lesson in this story? If so, what was it?

WRITING:

The writing focus for today is sight word review. Before the children write anything, tell them that you are going to be graduating all the List A Group 5 words to the classroom word wall. Post these words, then have the children facing the wall. Play Find and Write using these words (or other words from the word wall you feel the children need to review the most):

1. AND, 2. WILL, 3. BACK, 4. WANT, 5. BUT, 6. THIS, 7. CALL, 8. STOP, 9. COME, 10. SAID, 11. DOWN, 12. OUT, 13. HAS, 14. NOW, 15. HAVE, 16. MAKE, 17. HERE, 18. LIKE, 19. LITTLE

A fun variation on this game would be to draw names out of a hat and each child's name you call will choose a word for the rest of the group to write.

CENTERS:

Teacher Center
After reviewing student journals, read today's book together. Pay careful attention to any particular problems each child might be having, jotting down notes so you can pull groups together to review those concepts. You might have a small group of children who need more sight word review. Another group might need more practice decoding, etc.

When you have read the book, study the word wall with the children. Ask them to each find one word they are not sure about. Use your knowledge of their individual reading to choose words to review. If there are words they are struggling with, revisit the stylized side and ask the children to talk about the picture with you again.

Use R158 to have the children fill in the blanks in sentences using Group 5 sight words.

Reading Center:
Children will read today's book to their partners. After reading today's book, each child will choose another book to read to their partner.

Sentence / Picture Match:
Use R159.

Journal:
Children will write and illustrate their work in their journals.

Story Sequencing:
Use R160.

Review & Assessment

OBJECTIVES
1. To review & assess knowledge of sounds
2. To review & assess decoding
3. To review & assess sight words
4. To assess reading fluency
5. To assess comprehension

MATERIALS
1. Materials in Appendix C
2. Skills Tracking Form, section three
3. Independent centers, well stocked

FORMAT

There are three types of assessments you will be doing. Assessments are designed to spread out over three days. You will start each day with whole group assessments, move next to small group assessments on days 1-2, and finally on the third day, during small group, you will be doing individual assessments.

WHOLE GROUP ASSESSMENTS

Whole group assessments consist of sight word and sounds assessments. Prepare for this portion by dating then photocopying the student answer sheets. We suggest doing all the assessments on the answer sheet before grading any of it so the students will not be distracted by looking at what they might have missed the prior day.

SMALL GROUP ASSESSMENTS

After doing the whole group assessments for each day, break into centers. One center should be stocked for review of concepts you feel your students need reinforced.

In the teacher center on days one and two, you will be assessing in small groups in the area of phonemic manipulation and in listening comprehension.

INDIVIDUAL ASSESSMENTS

On day three, you will still have a whole group assessment to do, but when you break up into small groups for centers, the group at the teacher center will be doing individual assessments in reading accuracy and fluency. Be prepared for this center by having reading material or other silent review activities for the waiting children to do. Each assessment consists of two one-minute timed readings, so the waiting children might want to just silently cheer their classmate on.

Answer sheets, or teacher recording sheets are formatted so that they can serve as an accompaniment to the regular report card, should you wish to photocopy student scores and share with their parents.

INDEPENDENT CENTERS

It will be very important for you to have the ability to focus on the group or individual you have in front of you during this period of assessing the growth of your children. To this end, the more engaging the centers, the better! Some centers can be for review. Other ideas:

Silly Stories:
Take the picture cards that correspond to each sound learned, photocopy on card stock, then laminate them, and place in a bucket in the middle of a table. Instruct the children to randomly choose 3-5 picture cards and use them in a silly story. The two conditions for this activity are that they cannot look while selecting cards, and they must use all the words they chose in their little story.

Post Office:
Make available in a center attractive writing materials, stickers, envelopes, and let the children take time to write notes for someone. Encourage them to use the word wall as needed, and then to illustrate their letter if desired.

Story Writing:
Cut pictures out of magazines that evoke storylines and challenge the children to choose one to make up a story about. For instance, if there is a picture that is part of an ad for laundry detergent, there might be a child who has a lot of grass stains on his/her clothing. The story could be about what the child was doing -- maybe playing on a soccer team? These stories could be collected and made into a class magazine or book.

Switcheroo:
Supply the children with small cards and writing materials. Each child will be assigned a partner for this center. Each will make up sentences, writing one word per card, then will place the words in a snack bag and give to the partner to unscramble. Each child will make a sentence and solve one.

Word Match-Up:
Using two different colored markers, make sets of words that could form compound words. The first word in the compound word might always be blue, while the second word might be green. Children will take a baggie of about 10 words (enough to make 5 compound words) and match a word of each color so that all words are used. Ideas: sandbox, treehouse, baseball, sunshine, snowball, inside, nobody, daytime, playtime, naptime, lunchbox, tomboy, doghouse, dugout, cannot, cockpit, football, into, hilltop, herself, himself, myself, upset, tryout, today, suntan, starfish, snowman, snowball.

Art Center:
Supply each group with a large poster board sized paper and ask them to make a mural of themselves playing together at school or at the park or beach. There are many other ideas for small group murals: drawing the solar system, life in the time of dinosaurs, the world under the sea, going places (children would each draw themselves in their chosen vehicle).